The th

# The thinker

Thoughts from the heart of an evangelist

**Roger Carswell**

Authentic

To all who have prayed for the work of evangelism in which I am engaged, I dedicate this book. You are so much a part of my ministry that I feel deeply indebted to you for your help and participation in the great work of proclaiming the gospel.

Paul wrote to the Corinthian church the sentiment that I feel two thousand years later: . . . 'as you help us by your prayers. Then many will give thanks on our behalf for the gracious favour granted us in answer to the prayers of many' (2 Cor. 1:11, NIV).

In the verse we read of
       many people being blessed . . .
         and many people giving thanks . . .
           because many people had been praying.

# Contents

# Contents

# Acknowledgements

I am grateful for all who have helped me putting together this book. Many grateful thanks to Janice Bowman and Hannah Peace who unstintingly gave their time to help in the typing of the manuscript. I am thankful to Emma Balch who made so many helpful comments about the script, not all of which I listened to, so all errors or misjudgements are only mine. Thanks, too, to Jonathan Carswell who patiently and persistently nudged me onwards in moving this idea into becoming a book. I am grateful too, to my mother, who is not only a great mum, but a good proof reader. I am thankful to Hugh Palmer, not only for his kind foreword, but also his godly ministry. Most of all, thanks to Dot, my incredibly patient wife, who on those rare occasions when I have been based at home, has put up with me working behind a computer screen. Her reward in heaven will be great indeed.

# Foreword

I imagine that Roger has lost track of the number of short articles he has written over the years. I have read a fair number now and always look forward to them, for he has an ability to write even about familiar themes with freshness. He is a passionate, warm, enthusiastic and blunt evangelist. None of those qualities seem to go missing when he starts writing!

In the ten years or so that I have known Roger I have come to value the warmth of his friendship, his servant-heartedness and the way he gives of himself to his ministry as an itinerant evangelist. (Like most of his friends, and his doctor, I have probably also begun to despair of him listening to any wise advice about pacing himself etc. Such wisdom rarely cuts much ice with passionate evangelists!) So it comes as no surprise that these articles can make for uncomfortable reading and leave me with a new sense of urgency to make the gospel of Jesus more widely known.

Of course, Roger is passionate about what he writes and these articles spring both from a real desire to call Christians back to essential gospel-centred ministry, and the confidence to face us with our own practices or lack of them – whether that is our expectations or our disciplines – and try and hold God's Word up as a mirror to them. Even when he picks up on one of his favourite topics, tracts, you finish the article suspecting there is more to this than just a bee in Roger's bonnet.

Like several other evangelists, Roger seems to have a rich store full of snippets of information from all kinds of sources. Quotes appear from the likes of Goethe and William Morris, as well as the more predictable Hudson Taylor. He has the knack of making some easily missed points (John on his mentor John), getting under the skin with challenges (Great expectations), or just leaving you with a phrase to unsettle ('hear the voice of our neighbours more than the voice of God').

These articles are all short and readable. It would be easy to sit down and read them all at one go. Don't! It would be too much like scoffing a whole box of chocolates! Take them one at a time and let them do their work. These aren't designed simply to satisfy a sweet tooth or provide some short-lived delight. The subject matter is too important and the need too great for that.

*Canon Hugh Palmer*
*Rector, All Souls Church, Langham Place*

# Introduction

After eleven years of teaching in secondary schools, I began work as a full-time itinerant evangelist (though I dropped the word 'itinerant' after someone wrote to me saying, 'Dear *illiterate* evangelist . . .'). During my time as a teacher I had spent most evenings and weekends in evangelistic work; but God was clearly laying on my heart the burden to give all my time and energy to proclaiming the good news of Jesus. It had been the passion of my life since my conversion to Christ in 1965. To leave teaching, which I (usually) loved, seemed an enormous step at the time.

I decided to work as an independent evangelist, simply because so few churches or organisations employed evangelists. I talked with some of these but each wanted me to concentrate my efforts on students, or young people, or a particular church, or in the Yorkshire area where I live. I felt that the Lord would have me be available to all types of people in many situations. However, I felt so convinced that God really was calling me to be an evangelist, I took the decision to work independently. Without appealing to people, I would look to the Lord to open doors of opportunity and provide what I needed. To me, though I respect those who feel differently, it would have been demeaning to ask – or even drop hints – for preaching opportunities, or for finances. If God really did want me in the work, He would supply my needs.

When I commenced this new period in my life, one of full-time evangelistic ministry, I started to send out a quarterly prayer letter, sharing what had been going on, as well as making known the plans for the future weeks. People have faithfully prayed, for which I am hugely grateful. I wanted in turn to minister to my prayer supporters, and so would write a 'back-page article' which would seek to minister as I both expounded the Scriptures and shared the burdens of my heart. For me, these expressions of my mind are something that I prayerfully and carefully consider and work on. They are not page fillers, nor are they a systematic theology. There are particular emphases, because they are an outpouring of my passions. Others have written more thoroughly than I could on issues covering the balance of Christian living. Each is written in the context of the back of a prayer letter, to people who are prayer partners in the work of evangelism. Therefore, it has always been encouraging when I have had requests that they be used again in church magazines, missionary letters and so on. I recall, for example, J. Neville Knox, the Chief Executive of Harrogate Borough Council, and a tireless evangelist, sent a photocopy of the article entitled 'The thinker' to a hundred Christian leaders, little knowing that in just a few weeks he would be taken home to heaven.

My prayer is that God would take these articles and use them to speak afresh to your heart. There is such a need in these days, where society is so antagonistic to the Christian message, to live like Christ by spending much time with Him, and then making Him known to all. I hope some chapters comfort you, but others leave you feeling uncomfortable! I pray that they will glorify God. If you would like to receive my current prayer letter with its latest article, do send your postal address to me: Carswell77@aol.com.

# Mad dogs and Englishmen

On holiday in the Lebanon, 25 August 1965 was the greatest day of my life. It was the day for which I was born, the day I got right with God. The moment I asked Jesus Christ to become my Lord and my Saviour was like a hinge, for it changed the whole direction of my life.

I was brought up in a God-fearing home. My maternal grandfather had been an evangelist in the Middle East and was greatly used by God before his sudden death from malaria in 1945.[1] My grandfather was Armenian, my grandmother Greek. They lived in Turkey until the 1915 Turkish genocide against the Armenians. Then they fled to Syria (where my mother was born) and eventually settled in the Lebanon as refugees. It was there that my mother was brought up. My Yorkshire father later met my mother in Beirut during World War Two. He married her and they returned to England, where they deliberately bought a house near a Methodist chapel and thoroughly involved themselves in all it was doing. So when I was born in 1950 life revolved around school, home and church. We had family Bible reading and prayer each morning, though I never remember hearing or understanding the gospel. My parents were lovely people, devout, and full of integrity. They faithfully prayed for me. Sadly, their church was not really preaching the Bible or the gospel.

As a young teenager, I drifted from church, much to the grief of my parents. Friends in the boys' grammar school I attended were not at all Christian, and I was influenced by them. Yet I wanted to know about God and had a sensitive conscience, but found church irrelevant to me. Without God in my life I began going the way of all my friends, and that was not the way the Lord wanted me to go.

I had been to the Lebanon before with my parents, but when I was fifteen I was given the holiday of a lifetime as I went to spend the summer with my relatives there. It wasn't an easy journey to make by myself, but I got there, and had a wonderful few weeks. I played tennis, baseball, cricket and croquet with my ten cousins. We enjoyed the Mediterranean sun, and loved swimming and diving in and out of a nearby hotel swimming pool. Perhaps Noël Coward was right, for this Englishman, like mad dogs, loved the midday sun.

While there, a cousin asked me if I was 'saved'. I didn't really understand what the term meant, so I replied that I was. However, I began to want whatever it was that I saw these families had in their lives. My relatives had founded and ran a Christian hospital in the Lebanon, the Christian Medical Centre in Beirut. They were thoroughly gospel-loving people. My uncle, an Armenian Congregational church minister, one day arranged to play tennis with me. I remember that he wasn't very fit, but he was trying to build a bridge to me. After the game he began chatting with me about Christ. I was eager to know more, and eventually we sat on a log, in a clearing in the woods where we used to have barbecues. Opening his Bible he went through a series of verses in the book of Romans, explaining the good news of Jesus.

For all have sinned and fall short of the glory of God. (Rom. 3:23)

For the wages of sin is death, but the gift of God is eternal life through Jesus Christ our Lord. (Rom. 6:23)

God demonstrates His love toward us, in that while we were still sinners, Christ died for us. (Rom. 5:8)

. . . whoever calls on the name of the LORD shall be saved. (Rom. 10:13)

He clearly explained that God had taken the wrong of which I was guilty, and laid it on Jesus. He had died carrying on Himself my sin, and paid the penalty that it would have taken me all eternity to pay. Then my uncle, Revd Hagop Sagherian, asked me if I had ever trusted Jesus to forgive me and live as Lord in my life. I knew I hadn't, but thought that if Christ loved me enough to die for me, then the least I could do was to trust Him as my Lord and Saviour. My uncle warned me that it could be very hard to be a follower of Jesus, but I knew I really did want Him to make me right with God. I prayed with my uncle, thanking God for loving me, telling Him that I was sorry for my sin and wanted to turn from it, and asking Him to forgive me, invited the Holy Spirit to come and live within me. I meant every word, though I was only a teenager.

He changed my life: my vocabulary, my habits, aims and ambitions, and the direction of how I was living. I have never for a moment regretted receiving the gift of a new life in God.

I have not been back to the Lebanon, but I have never forgotten my time there over forty years ago. The Lord worked in my heart so that I immediately wanted everyone to know the good news of Jesus. It has been the passion of my life to share with all I possibly can the message of 'Christ and Him crucified'. Back home in Yorkshire, a youth group called Young Life led by Professor Verna Wright, 'found' me and began to care for me and nurture me spiritually, and I started to grow in my understanding of God and His ways.

God has not only been faithful to me, He has been overwhelmingly kind, incredibly merciful, consistently good and unbelievably patient: 'whom having not seen [I] love' (1 Pet. 1:8). I thank Him for saving me, and then for calling me into the work of evangelism.

# Section 1

# Our relationship with God

In witnessing I tell people about the relationship they can have with God through Christ. It is an appealing concept. Yet strangely, it appears that as Christians we find it hard to enjoy this relationship when we talk with God in prayer.

I trust these chapters will act as a pep pill to make us more prayerful people. The idea that 'prayer changes things' is not really accurate. God changes things, but we speak to Him in prayer; He hears, and He answers. What a God we have, and what a privilege we neglect if we don't pray.

The daily, dogged, delightful duty of meeting with God, reading His Word, singing His praise and praying, is the key to growing in our Christian faith. What an immense privilege is ours to be able to speak with our heavenly Father, the Lord of all. With much prayer there will be much blessing, but with little prayer, what can we expect? I am sure prayerlessness hurts the heart of our heavenly Father as it declares that we feel we can cope without Him.

In these next chapters, we will think about prayer, as well as concentrating our thoughts on the Lord, and what it means to grow in our knowledge of Him, as well as our love and devotion to Him. We want Him to increase, and in all things have the pre-eminence.

# Where have you been today, Jean?

I heard of a church minister who went to visit a bedridden, elderly member of the church. He made his way through to her room, knocked on her door, and entering asked the question, 'Where have you been today, Jean?'

Though she had been lying in her bed for months, her reply was, 'To the heart of Africa, South America and the Far East!' More radiance was on her face than would normally be seen on the most tanned image of a returning holidaymaker. But Jean had been on her daily travels, praying for Christian work and evangelism in far-flung parts of the world.

I knew of a lady who was a light sleeper, so each night she brought before God the names, families and work of many Christians scattered all over the world. After her death, her prayer book, with over eight hundred names of individuals (not including their families) who were prayed for regularly, was divided between a group of people who would continue to pray for them each day.

If we fail to pray, we have forgotten what it means to be a Christian, for a Christian is someone who has a relationship with God. We are commanded to pray, and are given instructions as to how to pray, but let us remember what a privileged and influential position we are in when we pray. There are times when I would like to bend the ear of our Prime Minister or royal family, but, understandably, they don't want to listen to me. But my loving, caring heavenly Father does want to hear my petitions. He is attentive to my every whisper. What a huge honour that God invites me to speak to Him, and to do so boldly.

There are places in the world I would love to go and preach the gospel. I will probably never make it there. I read of the huge and neglected needs of countries like Kazakhstan, Uzbekistan, Turkmenistan, Kyrgyzstan, Azerbaijan, Armenia and Tajikistan (countries my computer spellchecker does not even recognise!), all in just one small part of the world, and wonder what I can ever do to help them. But Jesus says, 'The harvest is so great, but the workers are so few. So pray to the Lord who is in charge of the harvest; ask Him to send out more workers for his fields' (Mt. 9:37,38, NLT).

There are rulers of nations who are making huge mistakes which affect the lives of millions. At times I feel like a bystander impotently watching as foolish leaders give their instructions that lead to disaster in so many ways for so many people. Then the Omnipotent Lord God, who rules over all, says, 'I urge you then, first of all, that requests, prayers, intercession and thanksgiving be made for everyone – for kings and all those in authority, that we may live peaceful and quiet lives in all godliness and holiness' (1 Tim 2:1,2, NIV).

There are people I see and meet, as well as teeming masses in Europe, Asia, Africa, Australasia and the Americas, who need to know that Christ died for them and commands them to repent and believe, and I am concerned that they may never hear. Then the Word of God reminds me that Jeremiah was told to pray to the Babylonians, Moses prayed for his rebellious people, and that Paul prayed for his wayward fellow countrymen, saying, 'My heart's desire and prayer to God for Israel is that they might be saved' (see Jer. 29:7; Num. 11:1,2; Rom. 10:1).

There are missionaries serving Christ faithfully, miles from home and family, and I know how it hurts when I am away from my loved ones for just a few weeks. They want the Lord to bless and use their work. Perhaps they feel weary, and while longing to do a long-term work, may have to curtail their work because of family, health, relational or financial pressures, and I feel powerless to help. Then the God who is known for His loving-kindness points me to Paul's words: 'you also helping together in prayer for us, that thanks may be given by many persons on our behalf for the gift granted to us through many' (2 Cor. 1:11). The verse has many people praying and many people thanking, because many people were blessed.

There are church situations where God is doing a great work and people are being saved, built up and sent out to reach others with the gospel. I would love to be part of them, and enjoy the blessing. In other situations, churches are struggling, squabbling or stagnating, and I feel I wish I knew what to do to help. There are pastors, evangelists and church leaders with whom I want to be involved, but time and energy are limited. Then the Head of the Church brings to mind the prayer prayed for a church long ago

> that He would grant you, according to the riches of His glory, to be strengthened with might through His Spirit in the inner man, that Christ may dwell in your hearts through faith; that you, being rooted and grounded in love, may be able to comprehend with all the saints what is the width and length and depth and height – to know the love of Christ which passes knowledge; that you may be filled with all the fullness of God. (Eph. 3:16–19)

There are brothers and sisters in Christ who are suffering dire persecution for their faith. I know that persecutors sometimes have become believers, yet in my heart I abhor them for doing what they are doing to people who love the same Lord Jesus whom I know and follow. Then the One who prayed for forgiveness for His executioners says, 'But I say to you, love your enemies, bless those who curse you, do good to those who hate you, and pray for those who spitefully use you and persecute you' (Mt. 5:44).

I am not a lover of travel programmes, for when I see them, I feel I want to go everywhere, except where the Lord has put me at that particular moment! However, in my prayers, I can, as it were, travel, but I may also impact the world. We know that the Lord intercedes for us, but we can pray for others, even if they never know of our prayers. To pray is not a device to excuse me from going, doing and obeying. When Isaiah's mouth was touched by the live coals of fire, the Lord commissioned him to go (Is. 6). A fire may burn in our hearts when we really pray, and the Lord will make it clear to us as to whether we should be going or staying. He has already spelt out that we are to pray, and as we do we can be certain that 'The effective, fervent prayer of a righteous man avails much' (Jas. 5:16).

# So, who exactly is praying for our nation?

The first sixteen years of my life, I lived on Vesper Road. Years earlier the land would have been part of the grounds of one of Yorkshire's many abbeys. Ruins are all that remain now, but they prove an attractive tourist site. To go round them and see the cloisters and chapel are a quiet reminder of something that has long since passed in the minds of most. I am not advocating the Catholicism that was the religion of the abbeys, nor the monasticism that in the bustle of our pressurised society can at times seem attractive. We know better than to pray to saints, or for the dead, or to use Latin or mysticism in our prayers.

However, when bombs went off in London on 7 July 2005, and a few days later Leeds was identified as the home of two of the suicide bombers, I began to think about the shame that had been brought on the city in which I live. I wondered what had been done to reach the bombers with the gospel (two lived very close to my home church). Then I wondered who in today's society devotes themselves to praying for our nation. I know from experience in my quiet times and in church prayer meetings I attend, that dominating the time is prayer for my/our personal needs, and those of people close to me. The 'big picture' prayer is left to Sunday church services, but even they can often overlook national and world issues. So who does pray for governments, rulers, situations of conflict, intrigue and national disaster?

There are more prayer letters and aids to prayer today than ever. We are constantly being urged to pray for one individual or another, but I still wonder if we have lost something by doing away with evening vespers, morning prayers, and unhurried time to bring to our ever-patient heavenly Father the needs of our nation. A friend with whom I was speaking on the phone, but who lives abroad, said to me recently, 'I'd love to have a week with you, just to pray and read the Bible together.' I'd like to take him up on that, but wonder where it would fit into my diary. Perhaps that is the problem, for I suspect I am quite typical.

**Just wondering**

I grieve over the 'lostness' and spiritual ignorance of everyday men, women and children. I feel for those who are devoted to false gods, following wrong religion and praying to non-existent deities. When I read missionary magazines, prayer letters and reports I am stirred. Yesterday, as an expression of that, I painted a picture of Yemeni people. It wasn't a great painting, and it certainly was not prayer. And then I wondered, who really prays for the lost souls of the Gulf? Who prays for the physically and spiritually hungry of Africa? Who prays for the untouched tribes, the spiritually misguided of South America and the teeming masses of proud, sophisticated, lost Europeans? God individually made these people; He loves them; Christ died for them, yet do I really pray for them? It concerns me. Where is the twenty-first-century equivalent of the abbey with its continuous cycle of prayers and vespers? There is no theological reason not to pray, so there can be no justifiable reason either.

I read in my newspaper of governments without integrity, of bad examples being set by those in leadership who should know better, of racism, prejudice and abuse, of bullying, abortion and violence, of divorce, immorality and permissiveness, of hunger, corruption and squalor and suffering, disease and death. I get so upset about the Christophobic bias of the BBC and media generally, the secularism of schools, the humanism (atheism, in reality) of the nation's intellectuals.

The hurt of these issues will either skew my emotions into darkness and despair, or I can bring them to the Lord, the loving Father, the Creator. He in His Sovereignty rules over the affairs of this world, and is 'not willing that any should perish but that all should come to repentance' (2 Pet. 3:9). Scripture says, '. . . I exhort first of all that supplications, prayers, intercessions, and giving of thanks be made for all men, for kings and all who are in authority, that we may lead a quiet and peaceable life in all godliness and reverence. For this is good and acceptable in the sight of God our Saviour, who desires all men to be saved and come to the knowledge of the truth' (1 Tim. 2:1–4). This is exactly what Samuel did. When the Lord confided in him the disappointment over Saul, we read, 'And it grieved Samuel, and he cried out to the LORD all night' (1 Sam. 15:11).

**Pass me my prayer list, please**

Of course, similar burdens are not new. Some time ago Christians took to celebratory prayer evenings for the nation, marches for Jesus, or walking around buildings and cities to 'claim them' for the Lord. To me, and for-give me if I am over-cynical, they seemed gimmicks, even if well-meaning ones. Should we not be just pray-ing? F.B. Meyer I fear was right when he said, 'The great tragedy of life is not unanswered prayer but unoffered prayer.' Today, prayer rooms are being set up that have graffiti walls, New Age type artefacts and other distrac-tions from biblical praying. Didn't Tozer write about the few meetings where the attraction is simply Jesus? So, let us pray! In April 2004, Prof. David Short, a Queen's physician and professor of medicine at Aberdeen University, went to be with the Lord. His final words, spoken to his son while lying in a hospital bed, were 'Pass me my prayer list, please.'

Let us pray in our devotions. Let us pray when we are with others. Let us pray as churches or Christian Unions or as friends meeting together. The Scripture seems to make so many of its promises concerning prayer to those who are praying with others. Let us remind our-selves, as the Operation Mobilisation 2004 Annual Report put it, to be 'More impressed with the greatness of God than the size of the task.' It would be wonderful if planet Earth would be a place from which the fra-grance of prayer universally and incessantly ascends to heaven, and that you and I were involved in that!

If you have not come across the books of Kenneth and Karen Boa to help your prayer life I wholeheartedly rec-ommend them. As well, I find praying through the Litany from the Book of Common Prayer to be very helpful.[2] The prayers cover issues I would normally overlook, but are nevertheless real matters for prayer in our troubled world. Better still; perhaps your church could have as part of its service from time to time, the Litany or similar prayers.

# Why worry? – reflections on Psalm 94:19

John Wesley said, 'I would no more worry than I would covet or steal.' After all, Jesus explicitly instructed us not to take thought about our lives, teaching us that worry is useless, needless and godless. Neither the birds of the air, flowers of the field, nor human beings gain by worrying. Anxiety is contrary then to nature, the providence of God and to His revelation. If we have really understood that God is all-powerful, and totally loving, what need is there to worry?

As Oswald Chambers put it, 'The child of God can never think of anything the Heavenly Father will forget . . .' Jesus never worried, and he said, 'Let not your heart be troubled . . .' However, although worrying is a drain on us, at times we find ourselves preoccupied with anxieties, cares and worries. We may not fret, but sometimes we are close to it. The Lord is aware of this, and so in His Word He has given to us the realistic, reassuring answer to worry. In Psalm 94:19 we read: 'In the multitude of my anxieties within me, Your comforts delight my soul.' The context concerns the pressure we feel through the apparent triumph of evil-doers, but let us note some things from the text.

## 1. I have numerous anxieties . . .

The world in which we live causes us to have deep burdens. We want people to be saved. We desire godliness
and righteousness in the land; we crave justice and
peace for all. Instead it appears that evil-doers multiply,
and break our hearts as they do. Also, we are not the
people we long to be. We fail to live consistently. The
most precious relationships can become strained simply
by our selfish desires. Time and again the world, the
flesh and the devil trouble us.

   All this leads to anxieties of one sort or another.


## . . . but God has numerous comforts

The twin themes that life is tough, but God is good, sum-
marise all one hundred and fifty psalms. Woven through
all the tapestry of life are difficulties and delights. The
hard times come from within and around us; the true
joys come from above. There is treasure in earthen ves-
sels; we may be hard pressed, but we are not crushed. In
the most testing times there is the greatest reassurance of
all: knowing a close walk with God, whose presence is
such a joy and so comforting.


## 2. My anxieties are very burdensome . . .

There are pressures that every individual endures. The
worry that a doctor may have some terrible news for us
or a loved one, or the feeling that there is just too much
to cope with, is common to all. As believers, we face difficulties peculiar to our relationship with God. For
example, we may be deeply concerned that a son or

daughter is not the Lord's, or that our walk with God is not as it should be. Consoling words from others do not lessen the heaviness we feel. Satisfaction can only come from God, but there are times when He can appear distant. Amy Carmichael expressed this feeling well

> Oh for a love, for a burning love,
> like the fervent flame of fire;
> Oh for a love, a yearning love,
> that will never, never tire;
> Lord, in my need, I appeal unto Thee,
> Oh give me my heart's desire.[3]

## . . . but God's comforts are sheer delight

'A bruised reed He will not break, and smoking flax He will not quench.' (Is. 42:3). Nobody would pretend that life is always easy, but we know that God's grace is sufficient. Whatever circumstances we find ourselves in, it is possible to know the overwhelming peace of our loving heavenly Father within us. A beating and a prison cell could not stop Paul and Silas praising the Lord. Get into the Lord's arms, rest and bask in His presence and you will find joy even in the most sorrowful situations. God loves to be called upon, so we cast our cares upon Him and relish the truth that He cares for us.

## 3. My anxieties are deep within . . .

There are burdens that are too deep to share with others, but even if we did, we know that their words would be inadequate to comfort and compensate. Job's 'comforters' would have been more eloquent if they had remained silent. Only God could answer his and their accusations, because only He knew what was really happening in Job's life at that time. When our concerns are so personal, so wretched, so heavy that no one understands, we need to be reminded of Psalm 94:19.

## . . . but God's comforts are for my soul

As we spend time with God, we see what a tender and compassionate Lord we have. His comforts delight the soul. In fact, He Himself delights the soul. There is a secret place where God will draw near to us and do us such good. There are times of refreshing to be enjoyed in fellowship with Him. There is no pleasure on earth to compare with the sheer joy of meeting with the Lord in undistracted communion with Him. An old hymn had the words: 'Oh, the pure delight of a single hour which before Thy throne I spend.' So whatever we may be called to endure, let us prove in experience the truth of our verse

> In the multitude of my anxieties within me, Your comforts delight my soul.

# Preying on prayers

I am not an Anglican. I was brought up to attend a small Methodist chapel where mostly lay preachers ministered Sunday mornings and evenings, and prayers were, as far as I can recall, all extemporary. Now, when at home, I attend an Independent church.

Nevertheless, I am aware that there have been controversies surrounding the version of the Book of Common Prayer. It has been my privilege to preach in churches that belong to the Church of England, Church of Scotland, Church of Wales and Church of Ireland. As well, by my own choice, I have frequently gone to worship in Anglican churches, and have been immensely blessed in so doing. I have been ministered to, and I am grateful to God. I have sung, listened and . . . prayed. I've prayed prayers that millions the world over, for several centuries, have prayed. In fact, on my shelf of most frequently used books I have a leatherbound Book of Common Prayer printed in the reign of Queen Victoria (I know that because the printed prayers are for her and Albert Edward, Prince of Wales!).

I find it helpful to kneel and pray the Benedicte Omnia Opera, or the Litany. For those who are unfamiliar with these prayers, let me explain. When I pray these ancient words, expressions of heart are formed in me that the selfishness, busyness and repetition of my own praying would overlook. For example, would I pray,

'That it may please thee to . . . show pity upon all pris-
oners and captives, to defend and provide for the father-
less children and widows, and all that are desolate and
oppressed' if I were not being reminded of these needy
people? Here's another petition, 'That it may please thee
to forgive our enemies, persecutors, and slanderers, and
to turn their hearts . . . That it may please thee to give
and preserve to our use the kindly fruits of the earth, so
as in due time we may enjoy them; we beseech thee to
hear us, good Lord.'

There are some requests that appear quaint, but I have
been helped as I have prayed them: 'From lightning and
tempest; from plague, pestilence, and famine; from battle and murder, and from sudden death, Good Lord,
deliver us. From all sedition, privy conspiracy, and
rebellion; from all false doctrine, heresy, and schism;
from hardness of heart and contempt of thy Word and
Commandment, Good Lord, deliver us.'

**Teach us *how* to pray**

The disciples said to Jesus, 'Teach us to pray.' I understand that request, for any Christian who is not alone
with God in prayer is in great spiritual danger. And the
Lord is so eager to hear our prayers. Sometimes, though,
I feel I have a more basic need: 'Lord, teach me *how* to
pray!' I know that heart is more important than words
when it comes to praying. I know too, that our prayers
are heard not because of anything in ourselves, but only
because of Jesus, and His sufferings for us. God heeds
inarticulate, impulsive prayer; but I find that too easily
my prayers spiral into a routine of requests that become
too familiar. Repetition in prayer is not necessarily vain
repetition, but it may reveal lack of imagination. This

may in itself be indicative of a loss of sense of the awe-some privilege of talking to Almighty God. There are depths of communion with God that I know nothing of. Eavesdropping on Jesus' intimate prayer to His Father in John 17 shows me how shallow is my praying. But then, Jesus was the Son speaking to His Father and I could never be like Him.

**Suggestions**

When I read the prayers of Abraham or Moses, David or Solomon, Asa or Nehemiah, Isaiah or Jeremiah, or Paul, it seems that every word of the great prayers of Scripture was carefully weighed. I have been with people who I have felt have an unusual richness in their communion with God. The Word of God and experience have both shown me that God answers prayer. I do pray, but I long to pray with new intensity, thoroughness and maturity. Hosea 14:2 says, 'Take words with you, and return to the LORD.' I want those words of mine to be the fruit of a heart which repents of sin deeply, loves God passionate-ly, submits to Him fully, and cares enough for others to bring them before Him in prayer. Do you feel the same? Here are some practical hints

- Turn Scripture into prayer (Kenneth Boa's books *Face to Face* (published by Zondervan), Vols I & II are very helpful tools for this).
- Use some of the carefully crafted prayers of choice saints to help you as you approach the Lord in per-sonal prayer.
- Pray aloud.
- Pray alone.
- Pray with others.

- But pray. Oswald Chambers said: 'Do it now, "enter into your room" and remember, it is a place selected to pray in, not to make little addresses in, or for any other purpose than to pray in; never forget that.' (If you need a lift for your flagging prayer life, read one of E.M. Bounds' books on prayer.)

And as you pray, remember the promises of God that He hears and answers: Psalm 9:12; 34:15; 37:4,5; 50:14; Isaiah 30:19; 58:9; 65:24; Matthew 21:22; John 14:13; 1 John 5:14,15.

# For this child I prayed

Sankey's *Sacred Songs and Solos* sold over 200 million copies. Today if we speak about that hymn book, we have a knowing, rather superior, wry smile because of hymns like

> Where is my wandering boy tonight
> The boy of my tenderest care;
> The boy that was once my joy and light;
> The child of my love and prayer?
>
> Once he was pure as morning dew
> As he knelt at his mother's knee;
> No face was so bright, no heart more true,
> And none was so sweet as he.
>
> *Robert Lowry*

And yet, the greatest sadness I come across in my travels is the bitter heartache of Christian parents concerned for their children. Every godly parent knows the earnest desire that each of their family should be committed to Christ and His service, but when this doesn't happen, heaviness of heart is a real and undying pain. Is there any more pitiful cry in all of Scripture than David's lament over his son Absalom, 'O my son Absalom – my son, my son Absalom – if only I had died in your place! O Absalom my son, my son!' (2 Sam. 18:33)?

I imagine the prodigal son's father going to the flat roof of his eastern house and looking to the distant horizon, longing to catch a glimpse of his son on his way home. Daily disappointment did not destroy hope, and eventually that hope was transformed into the most intense joy, and the old man ran to greet his repentant son. Yes, there were scars on the heart of the father, as well as the body of the son, but all that was in the past, and the son was welcomed and treated as if he had never been away.

## On loan

Children have been loaned to us so that we might love and enjoy them, teach and pray for them, as their lives are built in our homes. Even though things can go wrong, no matter how bleak the situation, the Christian has the wonderful hope that God can completely turn around the situation. William Grimshaw, the delightfully eccentric eighteenth-century vicar of Haworth in Yorkshire had a wayward son. A couple of years after his father's death, young Grimshaw was riding his father's horse on the moors, when a rather tactless parishioner shouted, 'Ay, and once a great saint rode on the horse, and now a great sinner!'

Young Grimshaw dismounted and with tears in his eyes said, 'Won't my father be pleased to see me in heaven?' He had been converted *after* his father's death. Until our dying prayers, parents are not to give up hope. (Doesn't John Flavel tell of Luke Short being wonderfully converted while working in the fields, aged one hundred and five?) God hears and answers the prayers of his people.

John sums up the attitude of teachers and parents: 'It has given me great joy to find some of your children walking in the truth' (2 Jn. 1:4, NIV). Hannah prayed that God would give her a child, and was able to testify, 'For this child I prayed, and the LORD has granted me my petition which I asked of Him' (1 Sam. 1:27). Job, aware that foolishness is bound up in the heart of a child, prayed each day for his children, in case they had cursed God in their hearts (Job. 1:5).

Children are a blessing from the Lord. We read that Jesus called children to Himself saying 'Let [them] come to Me', but referring to adults He said, 'compel them to come' (Mt. 19:14; Lk. 14:23). Little children can trust Christ and grow to be mature Christians. As the Scripture Union children's evangelist Hudson Pope said, 'Never under-rate the under eights!'[4]

## The greatest challenge

The challenge to us all is to pray for children. C.H. Spurgeon said, 'I tell you that in God's sight, he is no preacher who does not care for children.' The greatest care is to pray for children. It is an abuse of a child to be a stumbling block against them coming to Christ as Lord and Saviour.

Some years ago in Leeds we had a night of prayer for children. It was a blessed time, as some who gathered prayed for their children serving as missionaries, while others prayed for their children who were rebelling against the things of God. Shouldn't our midweek prayer meetings encourage parents to share their burdens for their children? Isn't this a very practical way in which the church can show its genuine love towards each other, by praying for the various families within the church? And while we have breath and time, shouldn't we plead with God to be merciful to our children? As well, there are children who live on our streets, and nobody would ever pray for them if we did not, so let us pray for children who otherwise would be unprayed for. As we do, let us remember that we are speaking with the Lord who said, '"Let the little children come to Me, and do not forbid them . . ." And He took them up in His arms, laid His hands on them, and blessed them' (Mk. 10:14,16).

# Swine, dunces and blockheads

'Swine, dunces and blockheads' was how Martin Luther described people who don't like children. He always was a controversial character! Whether *we* like children or not, they are individuals, having an eternal destiny, and are precious in God's sight.

Some years ago the Association of Evangelists produced a little card with the words: 'Pray for the unprayed-for child'. It came from the burden that so many are growing up in our land, and though they have more than they need materially, they are lost little children. However, they are often not told that, and few hear about how to be found. We are rightly horrified by cases of child abuse, but there is a consistent, systematic, thorough abuse of children spiritually by those who present wrong values and distorted views of the Lord and His work. Jesus was very direct in His warning to such people: 'Whoever causes one of these little ones who believe in Me to sin, it would be better for him if a millstone were hung around his neck, and he were drowned in the depth of the sea' (Mt. 18:6).

The burden for these children remains. It is the mainspring behind all those involved in children's outreach whether through Sunday schools, Bible clubs, summer camps, school Christian Unions, beach missions or ministries to street children. Whether or not we have children of our own, we can each be involved in praying for boys and girls. William Medlen Hutchings (1827–1876) wrote

> How kind was our Saviour
> To bid those children welcome
> But there are many thousands who
> Have never heard His name
> The Bible they have never read
> They know not what the Saviour said
> 'Suffer little children to come unto Me.'
>
> Oh, soon may the heathen
> Of every tribe and nation
> Fulfil Thy blessed word and cast
> Their idols all away;
> Oh, shine upon them from above
> And show Thyself a God of love
> Teach the little children to come unto Thee.

However, there is something else. In my personal prayer diary I have a long list of children for whom I pray. They all have one thing in common. They are all the sons or daughters of Christians. Many of them were prayed for when they were still in their mother's womb. They have been taught the Scriptures, taken to church, loved, admonished, encouraged, sent on camps, and yet . . . today, they are lost.

Job said, as he entered into his suffering, that the thing he dreaded most had happened to him. However, what Christian parents dread most is the spiritual loss of their own children. I have experienced the deep, prolonged, knotted feeling of heaviness over a child who is not walking with God. Nothing could be worse than the one we brought *into* the world being thoroughly *of* the world. It is no comfort to the parents when people say, 'Oh, it's just a phase . . . he/she will come back', for parents know that there is no guarantee of that. Neither is it sufficient to be able to say that the child is doing well academically, or has a good job, is happily married, or even that they go to church. The greatest concern is that the child would be saved, and evidently so. Whichever theological system we adopt, it is natural and right that our concern is for our children, and nothing of God should harden our hearts against them. Our cynical society mocks hymns such as 'Where is my wandering boy tonight?' but at least those who sang those words showed that they were concerned.

**What does the Bible say?**

I have a number of sermons on the prodigal son, or as Helmut Thielicke calls it, 'the parable of the waiting father'. As I have preached them, time and again my heart goes after the son, and I am amazed that the father was so patient. The father did not panic and go chasing his son, though I'm sure he wanted to. He waited and watched and, I am sure, poured out his heart to God whose omnipresence was in the far country too. The fact that he had one son at home in the fields was no comfort to him. His youngest son was living as if his father was dead, and that deeply pained the father. When the son eventually returned, the father was to ask no questions about how his son had lived; he was simply delighted that his son was home. His father's prayers had, at last, been answered. The son had eventually 'come to himself'.

There is no hint in the parable that the father blamed himself for his son's waywardness. Secret visions of sin soon harden the tenderest heart. Prodigal living can be like a cruel understudy hijacking the true person whom God has created. Every parent is aware, though, that he or she has not been as exemplary as they ought. We are all sinful and weak. Isn't part of the grief of David over his son Absalom as he cried, 'Oh, my son Absalom – my son, my son Absalom – if only I had died in your place!' (2 Sam. 18:33) that David knew he had been the catalyst of his family's problems? We may even be guilty of introducing our children to the wrongs that lure them, and now nothing in this world will hold them back from careless living, or hell itself. But even that does not mean that all is lost. I recently interviewed the son of a Scottish evangelist, all of whose brothers and sisters were believers. He had become one too, five months earlier, aged seventy-two.

Where we have failed our children, let us confess our sin to God and apologise to them (Prov. 28:13). Let us love our children, even when they don't love us and are behaving in an unlovely way. If they are breaking our hearts, what are they doing to the infinitely loving heart of God? Yet the Father sent the Son to seek and to save those who are lost.

Let us seek to use each opportunity to be with our children and to teach them the best things (Deut. 6:6–9). They may want to talk to us at the most inconvenient time, but they must always be a priority. Let us remind ourselves that the Lord loves each of our children and that where sin abounds, grace abounds much more. The Lord is able to reach even the most rebellious. Let us be encouraged by the conversions of Augustine, Dostoevsky or Franklin Graham whose parents' prayers were eventually heard. At the very least, they make us dependent upon the Lord.

## Above all else, pray

Above all else, let us pray for our children. 'Arise, cry out in the night, as the watches of the night begin; pour out your heart like water in the presence of the Lord. Lift up your hands to him for the life of your children . . .' (Lam. 2:19, NIV). Hannah prayed for a child, and later could say, 'For this child I prayed, and the Lord has granted me my petition which I asked of Him' (1 Sam. 1:27).

In our quiet times, let us pray for children. As we mix and mingle with them, pray for them. In our churches and prayer meetings, pray for them. If we can't share the individual burden with everyone, we can at least do so with discreet, loving friends. Pray that our children will grow protected from evil; that they will be hedged about from evil circumstances, evil people and evil influences. If they have drifted or become wilfully lost, we know God longs to welcome them home. Pray that our children will have Christian friends, or someone they will feel they can share with and unburden to. Could you arrange an evening of prayer for children? Maybe you could meet regularly with one or two others to pray together for children.

Jesus said, 'Let the little children come to Me, and do not forbid them; for of such is the kingdom of heaven' (Mt. 19:14). It is not God's will that any of these little ones should perish, so we can be encouraged to know that as we pray for them, our heart's desire is in tune with the Lord's.

# Unusual companions

I love a good biography, but I especially enjoy an auto-biography. I am aware though, that they have a danger of containing self-justifications, egotism and lies. Not so with the autobiographical snippets the apostle Paul gives us. He always has doctrine as the backdrop of information about himself.

The book of Colossians was written to encourage the Christians in Colosse to remain faithful to the gospel in the face of false teaching. In his letter, Paul first empha-sised the supremacy of Christ, then authenticated his authority as an apostle and evangelist by telling of his own suffering. He describes his sufferings in an unpre-dictable way: 'I . . . fill up in my flesh what is lacking in the afflictions of Christ, for the sake of His body, that is the church' (Col. 1:24).

I am not sure that I would dare say anything was lack-ing in Christ's afflictions. After all, it is the suffering of Jesus that has brought to believers redemption, justifica-tion and reconciliation. All that we have in Christ is because of Christ and Him crucified, so what could pos-sibly be lacking in the sufferings of Christ? Certainly, there is no deficiency in the finished work of Christ. So Paul cannot be speaking of redemptive suffering, and there is no way that he is referring to Roman Catholic notions of purgatory or the need to purchase indulgences, which would be inconsistent with the rest of Scripture.

Paul's sufferings and afflictions are distinguished from, yet identifiable with Christ's sufferings. Paul's sufferings are exemplary, but they, like the afflictions of every believer and every martyr, supplement the sufferings of Jesus Himself. All the afflictions and persecutions that are experienced for the testimony of the gospel, are a remnant of the sufferings of Christ.

**Lessons from history**

Christian history is the story of cycles of immense suffering, and what to us appear inexplicable traumas for the people of God. Thousands of the most devoted Christians laid down their lives, after years of faithful service, during the Boxer Rebellion in China. In the Troubles in Northern Ireland, a disproportionately high number of Christians were murdered. Many Christian children died in the massacre in Beslan. There are brothers and sisters of ours imprisoned in containers on a boat off the coast of Eritrea today – suffering only for their faith in Christ. There are situations where Christians live in poverty, or with unsatisfactory jobs, or in loneliness, or serving in areas where they are unappreciated, misunderstood and under pressure. Why does God allow this? What is His purpose when His children suffer?

Dietrich Bonhoeffer understood the inevitability of suffering. Opposed to the Nazi regime, he was imprisoned, threatened with torture and danger to his family. In April 1945 he was executed by direct command of Heinrich Himmler in the Flossenburg concentration camp. He wrote, 'Suffering, then, is the badge of true discipleship. The disciple is not above his master. Following Christ means *passio passiva*, i.e. suffering because we have to suffer . . . Discipleship means allegiance to the suffering Christ, and it is therefore not at all surprising that Christians should be called upon to suffer.' Dominic Smart says in his book *Kingdom Builders*: 'It would be an unusual plan for church growth that would read: "Disrupt your children's education, lose your job, kiss goodbye to your pension; then have neighbours turn against you and let the authorities evict you unlawfully. Get flung into prison. Have a few of your fellowship murdered. Then tell everyone how much God loves you."'[5] But the story of the spread of the church in so many parts of the world involves some of each of these things. God's ways are not ours, neither are His thoughts ours.

I was recently talking with Frank Brearley, the British director of the New Tribes Mission. He told me that in opening works in unreached ethnic groups, NTM missionaries go through personal suffering. It is usually physical, some of it demonic opposition, but in many cases it creates a curiosity among the people as to why missionaries are there, and why they stay.

So the afflictions of Christ are to be filled up by the reality of those who suffer, and are taking up their cross and dying to self. This is us as Christians incarnating to today's world the suffering of Christ. Martin Luther reckoned suffering among the marks of the true church. John Calvin went further, explaining that 'God does not call the people to triumph before He has exercised them in the warfare of suffering.'

> In every pang that rends the heart
> The Man of Sorrows had a part.

Peter, in his epistle, marries together suffering and glory (in that order), as being characteristics of the Christian life. 'Rejoice insofar as you share Christ's sufferings, that you may also rejoice and be glad when his glory is revealed' (1 Pet. 4:13, ESV). Warren Wiersbe says, 'Calvary is God's great proof that suffering in the will of God always leads to glory.' It did for Jesus, and it will for all who follow Him.

The Bible teaches that as Christians we have been entrusted with suffering, making the implication that suffering is a privilege if it is borne for the glory of Christ. That must be true if our afflictions are filling up what is lacking in Christ's sufferings. Dr Helen Roseveare, while being brutalised in the Belgium Congo after years of faithful missionary service, thought that Christ too was 'led as a lamb to the slaughter'. God spoke to her heart, 'They're not fighting you: these blows, all this wickedness is against Me. All I ask of you is the loan of your body. Will you share with Me one hour in My sufferings for these who need My love through you?'

So when suffering comes, we are to

## 1. Be strong in the Lord, but remember the value of vulnerability

Every Christian battles against human frailty, and experiences the suffering that are the marks of the submission to the will of God. We know what it is to be opposed, hurt, misunderstood, misrepresented, not thanked, used and abused, overlooked and discarded. Many of our brothers and sisters are desperately poor, unemployed, hungry, imprisoned, threatened, maltreated and isolated. The holy, humble suffering of one Christian, simply for righteousness' sake, is more powerful in declaring gospel truth than many a sermon or argument for the gospel.

And as we 'play the man' God may use us to 'light a flame which will never be put out'.

## 2. Rejoice in the Lord, but remember sensitivity to suffering

God withholds nothing good for those who walk uprightly. And in that we can rejoice. God is always a good God. He gives and gives, and gives again. Grace upon grace is multiplied to us. He has given us innumerable, exceedingly great and precious promises for this life and the next. But at the same time, virtually everyone is suffering in one way or the other. How much we know of the suffering of our fellow human beings is a measure of how much we love them. As Bonhoeffer said, 'A Christian is someone who shares the sufferings of God in the world.' We are to learn to suffer on behalf of the whole body of God's people.

## 3. Worship the Lord, but remember our witness to the world

We cannot separate the greatness of God, and the willingness, even desire, to suffer for His sake. Could it be that our spiritual ineffectiveness in the West is largely due to the fact that it is so long since we had our martyrs, or knew times of real persecution? This has led us to indolence, worldliness and prayerlessness. It is through the suffering of Jesus that we enter into the kingdom of God, and our suffering will translate that to our generation.

The apostle Paul was a chosen instrument to carry Christ's name to the Gentiles, but God would show him 'how much he must suffer for Jesus' sake'. In Acts 14:22 we read of Paul 'strengthening the souls of the disciples, encouraging them to continue in the faith, and saying that through many tribulations we must enter the kingdom of God' (ESV). Later Paul sent Timothy to the Thessalonians 'to establish and exhort you in your faith, that no one be moved by these afflictions. For you yourselves know that we are destined for this. For when we were with you, we kept telling you beforehand that we were to suffer affliction, just as it has come to pass, and just as you know' (1 Thes. 3:2–4, ESV).

So the filling up of Christ's sufferings is done on the long path from Calvary, to the empty tomb, to Jerusalem, Judea, Samaria and the uttermost parts of the earth. We need not fear suffering for it is helping to progress the cause of Christ, His church and His purposes. Our sufferings do not save us, for only Jesus can do that. But they supplement what Jesus has accomplished. Sacrificial disciples declare the sacrificial work of our Lord, and in this way we fill up what is lacking in the afflictions of our Lord.

# Even if He never tells me why

Charles Simeon, the eighteenth-century Anglican clergy-man, based in Cambridge, urged his students not to be 'System Christians' but 'Bible Christians'. I know what he meant. It strikes me as smug, and even arrogant, to think we can pigeon-hole Almighty God into neat packages that explain His character and workings. He is infinite, eternal and altogether wise. He is beyond the complete understanding of we who are finite, limited by time, and fallen, so that we often act foolishly. What we know about God is what He in His grace has chosen to tell us. We dare not impose on Him anything that is beyond what He has revealed to us. So, that often leaves us puzzled and wondering why.

Deuteronomy 29:29 gives us an insight into what our reaction should be to this: 'The secret things belong to the Lord our God, but those things which are revealed belong to us and to our children for ever, that we may do all the words of this law.'

The verse speaks of mystery and certainty. There are both secret things and revealed things.

## Mystery – the secret things

There are things we will never be able to understand, or explain. There are concepts and incidents that are beyond us. Things that concern God, or are permitted by God, or understood only by God, and overruled by God, are His affairs, and may be left with Him.

God is wise in His reservations, as well as His revelations.

I do not know any more powerful piece of English prose than that written by Jewish writer Elie Wiesel. He was born in Sighet, Transylvania in 1928. Aged only fourteen he was sent to Auschwitz and later to Buchenwald. Years later, he reflected on the first night in a concentration camp

> Never shall I forget that night, the first night in camp, which has turned my life into one long night, seven times cursed and seven times sealed. Never shall I forget that smoke. Never shall I forget the little faces of the children, whose bodies I saw turned into wreaths of smoke beneath a silent blue sky.
>
> Never shall I forget those flames which consumed my faith forever.
>
> Never shall I forget that nocturnal silence which deprived me, for all eternity, of the desire to live. Never shall I forget those moments, which murdered my God and my soul and turned my dreams to dust. Never shall I forget these things, even if I am condemned to live as long as God Himself. Never.[6]

How many of us, in times of despair, when all our dreams shatter before us, when pain in mind and body seems to consume our every moment, when despair and darkness overrides all the joys of living, and worst of all, when God seems distant, have felt similar feelings to Elie Wiesel?

There are so many familiar questions which arise as we go through life: 'Why did the illness come?' 'Why did the relationship fail?' 'Where did the sense of joy, and carefree optimism go?' 'What happened to all those plans and prospects?' 'Why is this wound so deep?' 'Why do I feel so alone?' 'How long will all this last, because I can't take any more?' 'Why do the righteous suffer so?' 'God, where are you when I need you?'

All these mysteries teach us

- *To be humble – we need to accept our limitations.* We are tiny, though deeply significant, creatures in a vast universe. The God who spoke and out of nothing framed the worlds, is well able to bring order out of chaos. He is altogether loving and knows what He is doing.
- *To be trusting – we need to accept God's will.* It may be that 'darkness is my closest friend' (Ps. 88:18, NIV). In fact in all the psalms, some of which express deep heaviness, never once do we read the psalmist saying that he no longer trusts in God. Gerhart Tersteegen said, 'As long as we want to be different from what God wants us to be at the time, we are only tormenting ourselves to no purpose.'
- *To be thankful – we need to accept that God knows best.* If God is allowing us to be hurt, He will not waste the time or the tears. He will redeem each, and use them for our good and His purpose. I love Henry Thoreau's statement that 'The things for which we visit a man were done alone in the dark and the cold.' In other words, what is happening to us in tough and lonely times is actually the making of us. Think about that and be thankful!

## Certainty – the revealed things

Despite all the unanswered questions and bewildering issues of life, we have the promises of God, which are totally reliable. God has revealed Himself; He has made Himself known. Scripture says, we know 'in part' (1 Cor. 13:12) but at least we do know! We know that there is a God. We know that He is infinitely loving. We know too, that he is our Guide for faith and life. His love for us is demonstrated by the death of His darling Son Jesus, who carried our sins on the cross. 'He who did not spare His own Son but gave Him up for us all – how will He not also, along with Him, graciously give us all things?' (Rom 8:32, NIV).

We know that Jesus has conquered death by rising again, and has ascended and is exalted in heaven. We know that one day Christ will return to His rightful inheritance. We know that we are safe in His care . . . eternally. Lord Hailsham, a previous Lord Chancellor who died in 2002, said, 'When I die and stand in judgement, I will plead guilty, and cast myself on the mercy of the court.' How wise of Him. It is only God's mercy, which secures our eternal home with Him.

Over and above all that God is and has done, 'He has granted to us his precious and very great promises' (2 Pet. 1:4, ESV). Just muse on John 14, or Romans 8 or Revelation 21. The old-fashioned Promises Boxes (ornate boxes, which contained little rolls of paper on which were Bible promises that could be pulled out randomly with tweezers) were too small to contain all the promises of God to us. Just think on this *one*: 'He will swallow up death forever; and the Lord GOD will wipe away tears from all faces, and the reproach of His people He will take away from all the earth, for the LORD has spoken' (Is. 25:8, ESV).

The things revealed enable us to cope with the things we don't know.

And the things revealed are told to us, not to gratify our curiosity, but that we and succeeding generations may trust and obey God.

I have heard a handful of sermons which to me etched an indelible impression on my mind. They are unforgettable. One such was from Steve Brady who speaking on John 13:7 (where Jesus said, 'What I am doing you do not understand now, but you will know after this') had three straightforward points:

1. Be glad for what you do know
2. Be humble for what you do not know
3. Be patient for what you do not know.

When my good friend Prof. Verna Wright was dying of cancer, he quoted to his daughter, who also had cancer, the words of the hymn by Dorothy Greenwell (1821–1882)

> I am not skilled to understand
> What God hath willed, what God hath planned;
> I only know that at His right hand
> Is One Who is my Saviour.[7]

God gives us an intriguing insight into His nature in Isaiah 45:15 where we read, 'Truly, you are a God who hides yourself, O God of Israel, the Saviour' (ESV). There is certainty here – God is our Saviour; but there is mystery, too – He sometimes hides Himself from us, but we can trust God in the darkness. Though God may be distant, he is never absent. He promises His presence and will never, no never, forsake us. This we do know!

Dr Helen Roseveare, missionary stateswoman and author, reflecting on her ordeals during the Congo Uprising in 1964 said, 'Can you thank Me for trusting you with this experience, even if I never tell you why?'[8] She had been brutalised, imprisoned and sentenced to death, but her thinking was right. God has revealed enough to make faith intelligent, but has reserved suffi-cient to leave us trusting in our big God.

# What to do in times of despair

In John Bunyan's *Pilgrim's Progress*,[9] Christian is on his journey from the City of Destruction to the Heavenly City. In an intriguing passage Christian falls into the Slough of Despond, 'a very miry slough that was in the midst of the plain; and they being heedless did both fall into the bog. The name of the slough was Despond. Here, therefore, they wallowed for a time, being grievously daubed with dirt; and Christian because of the burden that was on his back, began to sink in the mire.'

Christian was pulled out by Help who was then asked why the path was not mended. The reply came, that the miry slough was such a place as could not be mended.

This is true. Such sloughs can only be passed through. Depression, despondency and despair come over most of us. This is nothing new in the experience of believers. William Cowper attempted to commit suicide the day after he had written the hymn 'God moves in a mysterious way'. It seems that our toughest battles are with God rather than the devil. As Matthew Henry, the great Bible commentator expressed it, 'The God of Israel, the Saviour, is sometimes a God who hides Himself, but never a God who is absent; sometimes in the dark, but never at a distance.'

There are times when our heart's emotions are so deep that our prayers come from our innermost being in such a way that it is impossible to distinguish between crying and praying.

In Psalm 61, David's heart is wrapped in gloom. He feels cornered; he is no longer in control; it is as if he is being hounded and hunted with no escape. On this occasion it seems that his own misdemeanours had got him into this troublesome situation, and he had to run from Jerusalem. Thankfully he did not run away from God.

David's soulmate, Jonathan, was long since dead. There had been a time when he had come to David to 'strengthen his hand in God' (1 Sam. 23:16). Now David strengthened his own hand in the Lord, and prayed three prayers:

> Lord, hear me (v. 1)
> Lord, help me (v. 2a)
> Lord, hide me (v. 2b)

David's heart is overwhelmed, so he prays, 'Lead me to the rock that is higher than I.' This is a poetic and yet vague request, condensing into words the idea of what is actually required. This high rock speaks of

> Security – it is reliable
> Strength – it is formidable
> Stability – it is constant
> Significance – it is towering

David will pray again at the end of the psalm, but before that he brought himself assurance and took steps to remedy his gloominess. He cried to the Lord.

## 1. He recalls God's faithfulness (v. 3)

Each Christian is conscious that God is good in all His dealings with us. Friends of mine suffered the tragedy of their two-year-old nephew being knocked down by a car. As they prayed for him, they were aware that whether the child recovered or not (which, in fact, he did), God was still being good. Let us never forget God's merciful care for us.

> His love in time past forbids me to think
> He'll leave me at last in trouble to sink;
> Each sweet Ebenezer[10] I have in review
> Confirms His good pleasure
> To help me quite through.
>
> *John Newton (1725–1807)*

## 2. He re-states his position (v. 4)

David avoided the temptation to think of giving up on God and going his own way. Of course, it is tough to follow the Lord, but it is also right to follow Him. In time of trouble, to cease to pray is to become a victim of despair. Instead, David says that he will abide and trust in God. Verse 4 begins by speaking of the tabernacle and then 'the shelter of Your wings', which probably means the wings of the cherubim in the tabernacle. It is a lovely picture of the intimacy of the protection, which God gives to those who trust in Him.

By abiding in the tabernacle, David was not only where the priest presented the sacrifices and the laws of worship were fulfilled, he was also at the place where the manna was kept; where God's glory was, where no enemies could enter and where people communed with God. David was committed to this. Spiritually speaking, David was 'inside the veil'.

## 3. He reminds himself of his own commitment and service and of God's grace (vv. 5–8)

It is easy to think to oneself that all previous service is of no value. God remembers the cup of water given in His name and the mites given to His cause. One of the best uses of memory is to recall God's gracious handling of us, and how He has always met our needs, opening doors of opportunity. Then David remembers God's grace. He bathed himself in the loving-kindness of God. David and we have great standing because of what God has given us.

## 4. He reckons on the continuing goodness of God towards him, and on his continuing commitment towards God

Three times David uses the word 'forever' (vv. 4, 7 and 8). As Warren Wiersbe says, 'We are not to doubt in the darkness what God has shown us in the light.' So David can rely on what God has previously spoken (see v. 6).

David now ends as he began – by praying. His prayer is a passionate cry ('Oh!'), as he pleads for individual needs to be covered. He asks for mercy *and* truth, not mercy *without* truth. God is abundant in both, and neither is mutually exclusive of the other.

## 5. He rests calmly in the knowledge that joy will return (v. 8)

As Christians we know that we can sing, if not in this life, then in eternity. We will one day give to the Lord all the devotion and service which we now long to, and then we will enjoy His peace fully.

Ron Dunn, whose son committed suicide, tells of the couple who came to his church just to see if he smiled. Their daughter had been murdered, and they were reassured that Ron, maybe years later, nevertheless could smile. We can enjoy rest in God, and in the knowledge that all of time's trials will be eclipsed by the brightness of being with Jesus in eternity.

At another time, David could testify, 'We went through fire and through water; but You brought us out to rich fulfillment' (Ps. 66:12). And Isaiah says, 'When you pass through the waters, I will be with you; And through the rivers, they shall not overflow you' (Is. 43:2).

> Oh, safe to the rock that is higher than I
> My soul in its conflicts and sorrows would fly;
> So sinful, so weary, Thine, Thine would I be
> Thou blest Rock of Ages, I'm hiding in Thee!
>                     *William Orcutt Cushing, (1823–1902)*

# The footsteps of God

I have taken the overnight ferry from Hull to Rotterdam many times and have got to befriend some of the crew. There is always an apology that the ferry will depart late, but the assurance that all lost time will be made up. I have to admit, they keep their promise. Nevertheless, upon boarding, there is the knowledge that it will be fifteen hours before disembarking. It takes twenty minutes to look at my cabin, go round the various shops, visit each of the three decks and look at the menu (which is the same as the last visit – and always very good!).

It was nearly 11 p.m. and I was sitting in the lounge area listening to the pianist, eating an apple and reading a rather good book. Sitting at the table next to me were a couple of Dutch men. Impeccably dressed, they looked like two well-contented businessmen who had pulled off a good deal in the UK. They were sharing a bottle of wine and each smoking a sweet-smelling cigar as they talked and laughed. As I occasionally peered over my book, something inside me envied them. They seemed to have life sorted, with good friendship, and appeared to have no cares in the world. Life wasn't quite like that for me.

Within half an hour the scene had dramatically changed. We were now out from the cover of the Humber estuary and the North Sea was living up to the Force 10 gales we had been warned about. Bottles in the bar smashed to the floor and the people walking looked as though they were drunken sailors as they reeled back to their cabins. The pianist switched the piano on to automatic play. My two friends put out their cigars, finished their wine and made a hurried exit. Soon I was the only one in the Moonlight Lounge. I was still reading, but I had seen an illustration of a bigger issue. The true test of whether life has been sorted out, is not in times when the journey is smooth, but when times are rough.

None of us relishes suffering. We know that Jesus suffered on the cross for us, paying for our sin, but in the West we run from suffering and shun it. We ask God, 'Why?' and grumble when He doesn't answer. To remember God in times of anguish is right. To expect Him to satisfy our curiosity and tell us why is a mark of our spiritual immaturity. The psalmist reflected on this and wrote, 'Your footsteps were not known' (Ps. 77:19). In other words, though we know that God has revealed Himself, we do not know or understand all the workings of God.

God cannot be categorised or pigeon-holed. He is far greater than the fickle, finite understanding and explanations of our minds. We rightly deplore idolatry because God cannot be reduced to an image which can be seen or touched. Similarly, God is bigger than, and beyond, human understanding. What a compliment for God to make human beings in His image; what an insult for us to try to reduce Him to our image. But there is a contentment with the unexplained, because we know and trust the One who is in control. He has given us repeated promises that He will never leave us or forsake us.

## Unfathomable secrets

God has His unfathomable secrets. Sometimes we want to call God and tell Him that we are not impressed by what is going on. But the truth is that God, being God, doesn't need to explain His actions to anyone. '[God's] ways are higher than [our] ways, and [His] thoughts higher than [our] thoughts' (Is. 55:9). Job never knew why he was suffering as he did, but through it all God had not lost control. Job was silenced when the Lord spoke to him again. As one sufferer put it, 'I had a million questions to ask God, but when I met Him they all fled my mind and it didn't matter.' The psalmist felt his feet nearly stumble and his steps nearly slip when he looked around, until he went into the sanctuary of God and saw everything from an eternal perspective. Paul did not understand why his thorn in the flesh persisted, but millions have experienced what Paul did, that God's grace was sufficient.

Equally, it may be that the Lord is drawing near to bless us immensely and we are not aware of Him. When Abraham rested by the door at Mamre he saw three travellers nearing the tent. To him, they were tired, thirsty wayfarers. He had no idea that they were angels. Think too of dreaming Jacob, who did not know that the presence of the Lord was in that place. We recall Moses at the burning bush, Joshua before the captain of the Lord of Hosts, and Job saying, 'When he passes me, I cannot see him; when he goes by, I cannot perceive him' (Job. 9:11, NIV).

If prayers go unanswered, life appears unbearable, guidance is not forthcoming, dreams have all been shattered and God seems distant – God has not given up on you. The Lord does not always sound the bell to announce His presence, for that has been promised. As Matthew Henry said, 'The God of Israel, the Saviour, is sometimes a God that hides Himself, but never a God that is absent; sometimes in the dark, but never at a distance.' We walk by faith, not by sight, and that means there are times when we are not sure quite what God is doing, why He is doing it or where He is leading. But we continue in His grace to do what is right, and humbly walk with our God.

Joys in life for us as Christians are not dependent on a smooth ride, or even careful explanations. As Warren Wiersbe says, 'Explanations do not heal a broken heart, only love can do that.' God's way is 'in the sea, Your path in the great waters, And Your footsteps were not known' (Ps. 77:19). It is knowing and trusting God that brings life, peace and tranquillity, not in crossing our fingers hoping that the comforts of life will never be taken away. We may even find that it was in the storms that the Lord drew closer and carefully refined us to make us more like Christ, whom we love.

# God of the second chance

There is a famous photograph which captured the moment when Jack Ruby shot dead John F. Kennedy's killer, Lee Harvey Oswald. Never mind the political intrigue, the photograph saved the career of *Dallas Times Herald* photographer, Bob Jackson. While other photographers were snapping their cameras two days earlier when John F. Kennedy was shot, Jackson was changing the film in his camera. A quirk in history provided him with a second chance.

It was no accident when God spoke to Jonah after three days in the belly of the big fish. As a prophet, he had been clearly told to go to Ninevah and speak against the sins of the city, and warn of God's anger and impending judgement. The rest is history. He paid the fare to go on a ship sailing in the opposite direction. He disapproved of the Divine plan, and thought he knew better than God. His disobedience cost him dearly. Amy Carmichael applied the lesson to our situation

> Thou hast enough to pay thy fare?
> Well be it so;
> But thou shouldest know,
> Does thy God send thee there –
> Is that it all? To pay thy fare?
> There's many a coin flung lightly down
> Brings back a load of care.

It may cost what thou knowest not
To bring thee home from there.[11]


Three dreadful days imprisoned in the stomach of a
huge fish taught Jonah to pray again, and to submit to
the will of God again. Then we read in Jonah 3:1, '. . . the
word of the LORD came to Jonah the second time ...' God
did not say anything different to Jonah than He had previously said, but patiently He repeated and recommis-
sioned Jonah.

David committed adultery with Bathsheba, and then
was responsible for the death of her husband Uriah the
Hittite. It took a year before David came back to God. No
doubt he experienced the heaviness of heart that only a
backslider knows. But as he prayed Psalm 51, he found
mercy, grace and a new beginning. The words penned in
Psalm 23, 'He restores my soul' became fresh to him.

Peter was absolutely sure that he would never deny the
Lord Jesus whom he followed so devoutly. He firmly
assured Jesus that he would never deny the One he loved
so much. Within a short time the situation changed, the
emotion charging Peter's affirmation had died away.
Jesus had been arrested and was going to the cross. A simple servant girl pinpointed Peter as one of Jesus' followers, and Peter cursed and denied the Lord. Three times,
when Peter could have boldly shown his trust in Jesus, he
denied Him. Christ knew Peter better than he knew himself, and had a greater commitment to Peter than Peter
had to Him. After Jesus had been to the cross, been buried
and risen again, Jesus met again with Peter. Tenderly and
repeatedly Jesus gave him the opportunity to declare
three times that he really did love the Lord. In just a few
short weeks, Peter was to preach the first, great, Christian
sermon at Pentecost, and three thousand people were
converted to Christ. God is the God of the second chance.

I remember a godly old pastor once astounding me when he said, 'I've never been a disappointment to God.' I was somewhat taken aback, but he clarified what he meant: 'God took me on as a poor, wretched, miserable sinner, and I have never been a disappointment to Him!'

That does not mean that we can play around with temptation and sin. Rather, we are commanded in the Bible to shun all that is evil. The first Bishop of Liverpool, J.C. Ryle said, 'We should not expect sin; we should not excite sin, and we should not excuse sin.' He was right. Sadly though, we find ourselves falling short of being the men and women of God that we long to be. But the Christian life is a series of new beginnings, and there is always a way back if we are willing to acknowledge our wrongdoing, turn from it, and start again. God is the God of the second chance.

Every New Year, each new Sunday, any day is a time when we are invited to respond afresh to Jesus who said, 'Come unto Me, all you who labor and are heavy laden, and I will give you rest' (Mt. 11:28). I seek to pray faithfully for various individuals who once ran well with the Lord but who no longer follow closely. Each one represents a story of sadness. All the more, because there is no need for any one of us to keep a distance from the Lord. At times, we all act foolishly, selfishly and godlessly. The Word of the Lord will come to us a second, or third, or a thousandth time. And when God comes a second time, it does not necessarily mean that all we have is second best. God can restore the years that have been eaten by locusts (see Joel 2:25), and begin something wonderful within us.

The way back to God is the way we came in the first place. We come to the cross of Jesus where He paid for all our sin. There he paid the price for the sins that we have committed, as well as the sins of which we will be guilty. After all when Jesus died for our sins, all of them were future sins. The sins of our years as unconverted people, as well as the sins we have committed as Christians, were all laid on Jesus as He suffered on the cross. Through His death and resurrection we can start again, and He will give us the desire and power to live as God wants us to. We can find, as David did, that God restores the soul.

Jeremiah outlined to the people of God what the Lord required of them, and it is the same for us: '"Return, faithless Israel," declares the LORD, "I will frown on you no longer, for I am merciful . . . I will not be angry for ever. Only acknowledge your guilt – you have rebelled against the LORD your God . . . and have not obeyed me . . . return, faithless people . . . "' (Jer. 3:12–14, NIV).

Writing of Jesus on the cross, John Newton (1725–1807) wrote

> A *second* look He gave which said:
> 'I freely all forgive:
> This blood is for thy ransom paid
> I died that thou mayest live'.
>
> (my italics)

If we have been guilty of abusing the dying love of the Lord Jesus, let us return to Him and find forgiveness and the new start that He gives in abundance.

# The cross in 1 Peter

I have recently re-read John Stott's *The Cross of Christ*. It has been such a blessing to me. I have heard that there are those who teach that it is not necessary to explain the cross of Jesus when proclaiming the gospel. I'm not sure where these ideas come from. The cross is the centre, the foundation of all that we believe and are in Christ. So, I would encourage these people to read John Stott, or 1 Peter!

Peter has been called the patron saint of failures. Imagine how he felt, when out of sheer love for Jesus, he said that Jesus would never go to the cross, and Jesus replied, 'Get behind Me, Satan.' Peter had already left his well-ordered life, had begun to recognise how sinful he was, and see his true identity before God. But he had underestimated the severity of the battle, and what was really going on. He had yet to learn to trust Christ, and not himself. This was demonstrated when foolishly he said he would go to the death for Christ.

Later, it was Peter who had to be corrected when he had dared to say words that are contradictory, 'Not so, Lord!' when he was asked to take and eat 'unclean' animals.

It was Peter who had to be withstood to the face by the apostle Paul because he insisted on imposing Jewish regulations on converted Gentiles.

Nearly forty years later, in AD 67, after the apostle Paul had died, and shortly before his own death, Peter wrote to Christians scattered throughout the world, who were feeling the after-effects of persecution. It was years since Peter last caught sight of Jesus. Grace had refined his heart and restructured his beliefs. He saw the cross as all-important and as all-sufficient. Peter, who had been so impulsive, rough-handed and fond of action, was used by the Spirit of God to write the most tender and comforting words.

1 Peter is born out of much sorrow and many tears, as the author marries together suffering and glory. It is steeped in the Old Testament. Peter loves to quote, without using quotation marks.

He makes the cross the foundation of all he teaches. Peter has nine themes or waves of thought in his first epistle, but for each the foundation of the teaching is the cross. It permeates and saturates every part of his letter, even the greeting. This is my outline of the book of 1 Peter, and the last verse is the key to that section, which focuses on the cross:

1. 1:1–2        Greeting founded in the cross              1:2
2. 1:3–12       Blessing of being a believer               1:11
3. 1:13–25      Call to be holy                            1:19
4. 2:1–10       A living stone and a holy people           2:7
5. 2:11 – 3:7   Call to submission                         2:21,24
6. 3:8–22       Suffering for righteousness sake           3:18
7. 4:1–11       Call to practical obedience                4:1
8. 4:12–19      Suffering as a Christian                   4:13
9. 5:1–14       Christ-like pastoring and farewell         5:1

So the cross is the foundation of our

- Christian fellowship.
- The blessings which we know and experience as Christians.

- The desire and ability to live as holy men and women.
- The fellowship we have with God.
- The willingness to submit to and obey King Jesus.
- Our acceptance of and contentment in suffering.
- Our loving care for Christian people, as well as lost men and women.

As a mature Christian, Peter had understood the real meaning of the cross and this is what he proclaimed and underscored as he wrote to Christians.

Lecturing on evangelism recently, I was stressing the need in every evangelistic message to pave the way to the cross. Asked, 'If it is not in the passage, how can we?' (which is a good question if we are to be biblical preachers), the answer is that the cross is the backcloth or the context to all of Scripture. We wouldn't have 'In the beginning God . . .' if it wasn't for the cross.

There is a temptation to be cleverer than God is, and to move away from the foolishness of proclaiming Christ and Him crucified. Reading in passages such as 1 Peter (or 1 Cor. 1:17 – 2:2), we are reminded that

**1. There is an inherent weakness in the message of the cross – this sends us to God for His blessing**

Peter repeatedly speaks of the sufferings of Christ. Hanging on a cross in agony and shame was hardly macho or mighty. However, it is not the physical sufferings of Christ that atone for our sin, but that God laid on Him the sin of the world. This is the hidden work that no human eye can see, but is the heart of the gospel.

## 2. There is an inherent power in the message of the cross – this sends us to men and women for their salvation

> For Jews demand signs and Greeks seek wisdom, but we preach Christ crucified, a stumbling block to Jews and folly to Gentiles, but to those who are called, both Jews and Greeks, Christ the power of God and the wisdom of God. For the foolishness of God is wiser than men, and the weakness of God is stronger than men. (1 Cor. 1:22–25, ESV)

There is an offence to our message. Jay Adams says a Christian sermon is one that would cause you to be thrown out of synagogue or mosque. Of course, this is exactly what happened in the book of Acts.

We have no authority to harangue people. We are not to beat people with our words, or to be aggressive. I grieve over gospel preaching which comes across as if we are angry with the listeners. 'Be kind, you do not know what people are bearing', said the Scottish preacher John Watson. And he was right. As sinners, we are sharing with other sinners Jesus, the Friend of sinners. People are carrying sorrow, pain, shame and hurt; they bear intolerable burdens, have shattered experiences, crushed hopes and terrors of spirit, so let us be tender, compassionate, winsome and loving.

## 3. There is an inherent foolishness in the message of the cross – this sends us to Scripture for our authority

Our authority is not in our eloquence or creativity, but in what God has revealed in His Word. We proclaim Christ and Him crucified because Scripture does. Bishop J.C. Ryle said:

Let others hold forth the terrors of hell and the joys of heaven. Let others drench their congregations with teachings about the sacraments and the Church. Give me the cross of Christ. This is the only lever, which has ever turned the world upside down and made people forsake their sins. And, if this will not, nothing will. A man may begin preaching with a perfect knowledge of Latin, Greek, and Hebrew; but he will do little or no good among his hearers unless he knows something of the cross. Never was there a minister, who did much for the conversion of souls, who did not dwell much on Christ crucified. Martin Luther, Samuel Rutherford, George Whitfield, Robert Murray McCheyne were all most eminent preachers of the cross. This is the preaching that the Holy Spirit delights to bless. He loves to honour those who honour the cross.[12]

## 4. There is an inherent wisdom in the message of the cross – this sends us to any situation for their salvation

There is nothing to be ashamed about Jesus, or His cross. There is nothing of which to be embarrassed; there is nothing to hide, or disguise, or sweep under the carpet. We have the most glorious message. Our gospel is sufficient to meet the needs of each individual and every situation. God blesses the ministry which exalts His Son, and nothing so exalts Him as the proclamation of His finished work. So let us learn from Peter, and saturate our preaching with Christ and His cross.

# God, my husband

A survey in America asked people what they wished for when they blew out their birthday cake candles. Most women wanted more time with their husbands, while the majority of men asked for a better score on the golf course! Marriage relationships are definitely perplexing, though precious.

Though my priority in life is to preach the gospel to unconverted people, in my work I inevitably become involved with pastoral concerns. How many people face horrendous problems, are carrying burdens, broken hearts and bitter disappointments? In standing up to preach to a crowd, I never know how many hurts people are deeply feeling and what battles they are fighting.

Among the most traumatic has to be that of a strained or broken marriage. I have been with men as they have wept bitterly over the separation from a wife who was dearly loved. And I have seen women utterly bewildered by the unfaithfulness of a husband to whom they were devoted. For a man or a woman to leave their spouse causes the most grievous of hurts, creating the deepest resentment.

God uses this sad treachery to picture the wretchedness of those who belong to God, but who drift from Him or walk out on Him. '. . . "Surely as a wife treacherously departs from her husband, so have you dealt treacherously with Me, O house of Israel," says the LORD' (Jer. 3:20).

It is a common image in the Bible that God likens Himself to a husband, and the church to His bride. As people's minds are more like picture galleries than debating chambers, God is graphically impressing on us the intimacy of the relationship Christians are to enjoy with God: that of a husband and his bride. Such a human relationship is to be characterised by love, trust, intimacy and permanency – all features of our relationship with God.

## Life's hardest task

Being very honest, the hardest task (yet hugely rewarding, and such a blessing) I have ever faced is to be a good husband and a good father. I am naturally selfish, and to put others first, even though I love them deeply rubs against the grain. The Lord is not like that. He is not like us. He is infinitely good. He gives and gives and gives again. He has inexhaustible patience. God is depicted as a faithful Lover, but that leads me to ask if He is a jilted husband?

The Old Testament often pictures idolatry as adultery (Ex. 34:15,16; Lev. 17:7). There are times when our behaviour as God's bride is so wayward that it is betrayal and God says, '. . . she is not My wife, nor am I her Husband' (Hos. 2:2). God even writes a bill of divorce (Is. 50:1). The Lord's faithfulness to His bride is described through imagery and is then illustrated by the prophets.

We know that the prophets sometimes had to do strange things. Isaiah embarrassed people by walking the streets dressed like a prisoner of war. Jeremiah carried a yoke on his shoulders. Ezekiel lay on his side for one year and was commanded not to mourn when his wife died. However, Hosea enacted the most painful sermon of all. He was called to marry Gomer. In turn she gave birth to three children. Then she walked out on him. Was there another man? The answer is that she had many other men. She sold and spoiled herself as she became a prostitute. And she was a picture of God's people. As we read in Hosea 5:7 (and 6:7), 'they have dealt treacherously with the LORD'.

Was it weeks, months or years later when God said to Hosea, 'Go again, love a woman who is loved by a lover and is committing adultery.' God knew that if Hosea really loved her, then he would surely buy her back. Hosea stood in the crowd at the auction and redeemed Gomer with silver and barley. Isn't this what the Lord has done for us? Like Gomer was to Hosea, we are God's . . . by right (He made us) and by redemption (He bought us). He has redeemed us not with corruptible things such as silver, gold or even barley, but with the precious blood of the Lord Jesus. God is long-suffering and restores a faithless wife 'with great compassion' (Is. 54:6,7). He is warm and tender towards us, healing His spouse's faithlessness (Hos. 11:8; 14:4).

**Abuse?**

However, are we guilty of abusing the faithfulness of God our husband? Have we behaved like an adulterous wife? 'You are not your own; you were bought at a price. Therefore honour God with your bodies' (1 Cor. 6:19,20). Do we fail to cultivate the closeness we should enjoy with the Lord? Are we belligerent, stubborn or just plainly disobedient towards God? Is my chief delight to be with Him, to listen and learn, to admire and worship and bask in His presence? Is the sheer joy of young love fading through familiarity?

If Hosea depicts redemption, then the Song of Solomon depicts the relationship we have with the Lord and it does so in more intimate detail than any other place in Scripture. Union and communion are to be the normal order. In chapter 5:2 onwards there is the description of a woman who has gone to her room for the night. She has retired, having anointed herself with perfume. Then there is a knock on her door . . . her lover has come and wants to be with her. She hesitates and remains inside. She has gone to bed and does not want to get up. Then suddenly he leaves, and immediately she realises he has gone and she is left. All her perfume is useless.

What trappings keep us from closeness to God? Which sins have crept in and lured us to drift from Him? Or are we being wrenched from the Lord who loves us with an everlasting love? Has spiritual neglect kept us from revelling in His commitment to us?

Five times in Jeremiah 3 and 4 God says to His people, 'Return!' (3:7,12,14,22; 4:1). There is a way back to God from the dark paths of sin. God still commands and invites us to return. We need to

## 1. Come back to the Lord

We return the same way we came to begin with, namely by coming to the cross where Christ bore our sins in His own body on the tree. Even if our hearts condemn us as we approach Him, God is greater than our hearts and runs to welcome us (1 Jn. 2:2; Lk. 15:11 ff.). '. . . the blood of Jesus Christ, [God's] Son, cleanses us from all sin' (1 Jn. 1:7). The Christian life is a series of new beginnings and so in our Christian walk time and again we'll come to God and tell Him we want to begin all over again. In marriage I suspect that the most important words are not, 'I love you' – crucial as they are – but, 'I'm sorry.' The Lord is willing to wash away every sin if there is repentance.

## 2. Cultivate communion with the Lord

I have found in marriage that I have to make time to be with my wife so we can enjoy unhurried time together. There are demanding matters which are urgent, but surely this is to be a priority. Similarly, I need to make time to be with the Lord. The discipline of reading the Bible and praying has no substitute. That holy habit of a regular quiet time is a must. There is no joy on earth like meeting with God, but I find I have to do battle each day to ensure that it is *the* priority.

## 3. Keep close to the Lord

I thank God for His faithfulness to me, but that is no excuse to abuse His dying love. God's grace is great, but I must not flirt with sin just because I know God will forgive me. Where sin gets a hold let us quickly confess and renounce it, committing ourselves afresh to walk worthy of our high calling. We as believers are privileged to be part of the bride of Christ, and should seek to be without spot or blemish before Him.

# Section 2

## Our Christian life

In writing for my prayer partners I want to encourage and exhort to godly living. The themes covered are really quite eclectic, and represent what I had been thinking about over the weeks before writing the next page. Reading them now (some were written nearly fifteen years ago) I can see how I have changed (matured?). In many ways the themes are quite random, and certainly don't represent every aspect or joy of living with our Lord. I trust they will excite and enthuse you.

# Say cheese?

I have always been challenged by the words of Hudson Taylor, the founder of the China Inland Mission, when he said, 'If I had a thousand lives, I would give them all to China.' If I had so many lives, I wonder if I would be tempted, even if for just one of them, to be something other than an evangelist? Those who know me well will not be surprised to read that there is something within me which would quite like to try my hand at business. When the work of evangelism gets tough, I confess that I have allowed my imagination to dwell on alternatives.

I love cheese. For a while I even mused on the idea of a super-chain of take-away foods, offering different flavours of cheese on toast. I feel sure that 'Say Cheese' could be as popular as McDonalds or KFC!

Enough of dreaming. God has called me to something else. But I'm not the first to think like this. One far greater than me allowed his imagination to wander. The Old Testament prophet Jeremiah carried a burden which seemed unbearable and his concern for his people was beyond his ability to cope. From the depth of his heart he cried:

> Oh, that my head were a spring of water and my eyes a fountain of tears! I would weep day and night for the slain of my people. Oh, that I had in the desert a lodging

> place for travellers, so that I might leave my people, and
> go away from them . . . (Jer. 9:1,2, NIV)

A local wayside bed and breakfast could be a marvellous opportunity for a man to meet with travellers and indeed witness to them, but Jeremiah knew that he had not been called to run an inn. I am aware of some fine, evangelistic cafés and hostels. Hoteliers are well able to glorify the Lord in their secular employment, but not if the Lord has clearly directed them to something else. For Jeremiah to do anything other than being a prophet who would 'root out, pull down, destroy, throw down, build and plant' (see Jer. 1:5,10) would have been at best a dangerous distraction and at worst an act of arrogant disobedience.

To consider deviation from duty is not new. Moses made his excuses, Elijah ran into the wilderness, and the psalmist longed for the wings of a dove to escape the pressures and trials of life. Others' needs and our duties can appear overwhelming. The feeling of 'so much to do and so little time to do it in' can lead to despair. Frankly, seeing the sins of the world around and mentally dwelling on the lostness of the lost at times causes me inward, physical pain. But any sense of hurt should drive us to the Lord, not to the dereliction of duty.

As far as my personal fantasies are concerned, you will be pleased to know that 'Say Cheese' has not yet opened! I feel fairly sure that even if town planners gave permission for such a place, the ultimate Planner of Lives would not. God is, after all, 'the God of my life' (Ps. 42:8). However, there are times when it is good to ask ourselves if we have drifted away from what ought to be the main commitment of our lives. A former policeman explained the tactics of roving bands of thieves. He said that they enter a shop as a group. One or two separate themselves from the group while the others start a loud commotion in another section of the shop. This gets the attention of the shopkeepers and cus- tomers. As everyone's attention is turned to that distur- bance, the accomplices fill their pockets with anything and everything, leaving before anyone suspects any- thing. Hours later, when the shop owner discovers what has happened, it is too late. He has been robbed. Distraction is deadly.

We have only one short life. Sooner than we realise, the years will have fled, and the opportunities to serve Christ here on earth will have gone forever. All that we are or have or hope to be is to be devoted (afresh?) to the Lord who gave us His dear Son. Times may be tough, and the hearts of the people we are trying to reach very hard, but we are still under marching orders from our Master, and His arm has not become so short that He cannot save.

Jeremiah knew this, and within a few verses of his complaint, we find him again proclaiming, 'Thus says the LORD of hosts.' He was put in the stocks, lowered by ropes into the miry dungeon, mocked, derided, accused of treachery, opposed by false prophets, forcibly carried to Egypt and repeatedly imprisoned. But this man of strife and contention went on steadily delivering his message for over forty years. The word was in his heart as a burning fire shut up in his bones. To hold back from preaching the Word of God was a weariness in itself, and he concluded that he could not (Jer. 20:9).

God calls us each to different spheres of work, influ- ence and ministry, and whatever that is, is not to be our area of concern (1 Cor. 7:20,21). The Lord has scattered us that we might produce fruit wherever we are. Those in secular employment are able to be in daily contact with people in a way that those whose life-work is in 'full-time' Christian service do not necessarily meet. Whether 'over-timers' or 'full-timers', each Christian is called to proclaim the Word of God to the world. We are to live for Christ and seek to make Him known to everyone. We each need to ask ourselves if anything is distracting us from this supreme calling. Satan uses legitimate concerns as well as blatant sins to swerve us from the course of duty, which is the Lord's commission to us. But, nothing else is worthy in comparison to the overwhelming need to urgently reach men and women with the gospel. So whatever sphere of work God has put us in, we are to be reminded that we are there to serve and to proclaim Christ Jesus the Lord.

Whatever the cost or the consequences, surely we will want to discipline ourselves and arrange our priorities and plans so that our life's work is given to actual 'eyeball to eyeball' evangelism.

So, farewell to 'Say Cheese'. This life had been bought at a price, and is committed to glorying God in body and spirit, which are God's (1 Cor. 6:20). I have been to the cross, and cannot let anything deflect me from going straight forward.

# Thirst and foremost

The Lord who is on the throne of heaven wants to be on the throne of our hearts. He is the One who, as Lord of the harvest, is better able than anyone else to assess His children and any work for God. God is always close to His children, and although there are times when we drift from Him, His Fatherly eye is always towards us. Nevertheless, from time to time, it is good to take stock and ask ourselves about our spiritual life and our work for Him. Reassessment of all relationships is a valuable exercise. Spiritual check-ups concerning our walk with God are a vital necessity if our relationship with Him is to be close and our work of eternal significance. They guard us against the danger of drifting.

When the Lord assessed the church in Ephesus, He concluded, 'Nevertheless I have this against you, that you have left your first love' (Rev. 2:4). They were guilty of leaving – not accidentally losing – their first love. According to Revelation 2:2,3 and 6, the church there was sacrificial, serving, steadfast and separated, but intimacy between God and them had gone. The words spoken were to an orthodox, evangelical church which was in danger of becoming a carpet warehouse or worse! The church was told first to remember, and then to repent, and this command was repeated (v. 5). Because we know that a Christian who sins is still a Christian, we can be tempted to play fast and loose with God's grace. Though

God keeps His people however mature in age or spirituality, there is always a danger of losing our first love. In fact, as Christians, the more we grow in grace, the more we should be wary of losing our first love.

## No light matter

This is not an inconsequential issue. Bible words used to describe backsliding like this are those used elsewhere to condemn the most awful immorality. Francis Schaeffer said: 'Apostasy must be called what it is – spiritual adultery.' There is nothing glib about side-stepping, resisting, neglecting or dethroning the Lord. If we are guilty we are not in need of sympathy, but whatever it takes to bring us back to submission and fellowship with God.

There have been people who have disappointed the people of God. They once ran well, but something hindered them. However, rather than talk about *them*, we need to ask ourselves how is *our* walk with God? We need to give the more earnest heed to the things we have heard, lest we drift away (Heb. 2:1). The godly nineteenth-century Scottish minister Robert Murray McCheyne said that what a person is before God, is what he is and no more.

So, with a spiritual stethoscope in hand, let us individually consider ourselves.

## I have left my first love when

- I thrill about someone or something more than the Lord (Lk. 10:27).
- I am not longing for fellowship with God through His Word and in prayer (Mt. 5:6).

- The Word of God is supplanted by my human wisdom (Gal. 1:8,9).
- My private thoughts do not focus on the Lord (Ps. 10:4).
- I excuse myself for giving in to the things which displease the Lord (Jn. 14:15).
- I do not cheerfully give my time, money and energy to the Lord (1 Jn. 3:17).
- I fail to treat other Christians as I would the Lord (Mt. 25:40; Jn. 13:34; Rom. 14:15).
- The approval of the world dictates my actions, rather than pleasing the Lord (1 Jn. 2:15).
- I scheme to accomplish 'the purposes of God', forgetting that faith is living without scheming (Jn. 15:10).
- I balk at the commands of Christ seeing them as restrictions rather than expressions of God's love (Jn. 14:21).
- I fail to share the gospel with boldness and compassion (Mt. 28:18,19).
- I am unmoved by the wickedness and lostness of the world around me (Mt. 24:12).
- I refuse to forgive those who have hurt me (1 Jn. 4:20).

The list could go on, but the challenge is already in place. Christian living involves death to self, and is characterised by hungering after righteousness, and thirsting for the One who is altogether righteous. The purpose of self-examination is not to send us on a guilt trip, but to drive us freshly to the Lord, who alone can satisfy the soul. We want nothing to lead us to turn away from Him who called us in the grace of Christ (Gal. 1:6).

'The Christian life is a series of new beginnings', said Alexander Whyte, so let us obey the Lord, acknowledge our waywardness, repent of it and return to the Lord. The way back is the way we came in the first place. We bow before the Christ of the cross, and ask Him to wash us afresh, and fill us again with His Holy Spirit. What exceedingly great and precious promises God gives to those who humbly come back to Him! (See Jer. 3:14–22; Joel 2:25; 2 Chr. 7:13,14).

'Come . . . let us return to the LORD' (Hos. 6:1).

# As His custom was

I admire those who are disciplined at jogging three times a week or who get their money's worth from a year's subscription to the gym. I esteem such self-discipline.

When a person is born again, God does not give the new believer a fully-fledged series of 'holy habits'. Each Christian has to make those habits. Of course, there are dangers to having habits. For example, it is all too easy to become legalistic, fooling ourselves into believing that the keeping up of habits brings us favour with God. As well, there is a tendency to judge others by the standards that we have set for ourselves. There is a Pharisee in each of us, which only grace can conquer. And we have to be careful not to make a god of our habits. Only the Lord is God!

Nevertheless, it is right to have customs or habits. The legalism of a past generation must not be replaced by the license of today's. After all, we are told to 'add to your faith goodness; and to goodness, knowledge; and to knowledge, self-control . . .' (2 Pet. 1:5,6, NIV). '. . . the fruit of the Spirit is . . . self-control' (Gal. 5:22,23). Discipline does not buy or bring God's grace, but neither does it negate it. Self-discipline will lead us to have right habits, and to have good habits there must be self-discipline.

In Acts 17:2, we read that Paul, 'as his custom was . . .' This is Paul, a pattern believer, as a mature Christian, basking in the grace of the Lord, busily serving his Saviour, having habits. The man who had been a legalistic Pharisee demonstrates how to have customs without losing Christian freedom. Acts 17 describes three of Paul's customs.

First, he went to the synagogue. Paul led a pressurised life: he was preaching and discipling, tent-making and pastoring many congregations and people, *but* he still had the custom of going to the synagogue. It was a priority of his life. The Bible does not tell us how many times a week we should be worshipping with other believers, but surely, if we really loved the Lord, His Word and His people, we would want more and more rather than less and less corporate worship.

We are instructed not to forsake the assembling of ourselves together as was the manner of some. I understand that there is a substance present when the roots of trees touch, that reduces competition. In fact this unknown fungus helps link roots of different trees, even dissimilar species. A whole forest may be linked together. If one tree has access to water, another to nutrients and a third to sunlight, the trees have the means to share with one another. Isn't this illustrative of what 1 Corinthians 12 is teaching us? We are part of the body of Christ. We need each other and want to be a blessing one to another.

Jesus had the same custom. In Luke 4:16 (NIV) we read of Him that, 'on the Sabbath day He went into the synagogue, as was his custom. . . .' The customs of Jesus and Paul should be ours.

Secondly, Paul preached the Word (Acts 17:2). It was Paul's custom to explain, demonstrate, and persuade people concerning Christ's death and resurrection. In this setting, where he was with God-fearing people, Paul reasoned with the people from the Scriptures. He believed in doctrine without indoctrination. He used the

Old Testament as a bridge to Jesus Christ. For Paul, evangelism was a lifestyle.

Whether defending himself in court, attending a place of worship, incarcerated in a Roman cell or rubbing shoulders with people in the market place, he had to speak of Christ. It was his custom. It was a holy habit that came from the overflow of his heart. A short time later, Paul was in Berea, again in the synagogue, and again preaching the Word (vv. 10 and 11). Then when Paul moved on to Athens, there is a repetition of the same pattern: he went to the synagogue and preached the Word (v. 17). Like the psalmist (Ps. 96:2) he proclaimed 'the good news of His salvation from day to day'.

In John 18:20 Jesus said, 'I have spoken openly to the world . . . I always taught in synagogues or at the temple, where all the Jews come together. I said nothing in secret.' Christ came, not so much to preach the gospel, but that there might be a gospel to preach; nevertheless, His custom was to preach the Word.

Thirdly, Paul faced suffering (Acts 17:2 ff.). Some suffering is the calling of every believer, but especially those God calls to bear the gospel to the unreached. Goethe said, 'The deepest, the only theme in human history is the conflict of scepticism with faith.' That explains both why Christians have suffered, and the increase of suffering and martyrdom in parts of the world today.

Satan's attack in Thessalonica was against Paul and the Christians' faith. In 2 Corinthians 11, Paul describes his sufferings, which are immense. In Peter's first letter, he has the twin themes of suffering and glory. In the West, we have a notion that if there is suffering there is no glory or vice versa, but that is not God's way. Jesus, Paul, Peter, John and James each warned that great times of distress and opposition would come. It was Paul's custom to face opposition. Maybe our lack of power is partly due to the fact that we lack a spirit willing – if need be – for martyrdom.

Paul was following the example of Jesus who suffered. Jesus identified Himself with human suffering first when He was circumcised at the age of eight days. He knew what it was to be hungry, thirsty, tired, tested and tried. In the Garden of Gethsemane, He sweated great drops of blood. His blood was spilt on the streets of Jerusalem as He carried the cross. His friends, who once forsook everything to follow Jesus, fled and forsook him. Insults were hurled at Him. Eventually, He hung, suffering, bleeding and dying on the cross for us. We are not above our Master. We too must 'bleed' if we would bless others.

So, what are our customs? To quote Hudson Taylor: 'A person may be dedicated and devoted, but if ill-disciplined, will be useless.' Oh, to have scrupulous punctuality in our private habits. We influence the places we live by our ruling habits. As well, disciplining our body and bringing it into subjection enables us to live enjoying the freedom of friendship with the Lord, without offending Him. This is not legalism, but an attitude that says there are things that are right to do, and they are going to be my customs, for the glory of God.

# Sacrificing sacrifice

There are trends in evangelical thinking. Some are about concepts we emphasise; others are ones we neglect. Some trends delight me; others create concern. I am still shocked by how quickly fads come, cause immense fascination, create euphoria among a group of people, and then disappear like a vapour. How much evangelical energy is wasted in these is beyond calculation.

Since I have been a Christian I have noticed a diminishing interest in various challenging concepts. In fact, there is almost antagonism towards them. One example is the Bible's teaching on sacrificial Christian living. When I read missionary biography, I am reminded that missionary heroes of previous centuries were characterised by a separation from the cares of this world, the love of things and the deceitfulness of riches. They lived lives of sacrifice, which defied losses, setbacks and difficulties. Some worked in beautiful parts of the world, and could at least enjoy the beauty of the world around them.

Hudson Taylor, the nineteenth-century missionary to China said, 'I enjoyed the luxury of having few things to care for.' And hundreds of the best-educated in the U.K. joined him in China, laying down their lives in the cause of proclaiming the gospel.

University students from the UK and the USA went to Africa, knowing that in six months they would almost certainly die of disease. David Livingstone said, 'I will place no value on anything I have or may possess except in relation to the kingdom of Christ. If anything will advance the interests of that kingdom it shall be given away or kept, only as by giving or keeping it I shall promote the glory of Him to whom I owe all my hopes in time and eternity.'

A century earlier, the Moravians had missionaries who sold themselves into slavery (think about it!) so that they might effectively reach slaves with the gospel.

## David and the water of the well of Bethlehem

Today, for whatever reason all this seems to have changed, and sacrifice for Christians has almost become a forgotten teaching in the West. The life of King David serves to provide an illustration of the willingness of a child of God to give all to the Lord (see 2 Sam. 23:8–17). David was with his mighty men, but his fortunes were low. He was hiding in a cave of Adullam as the Philistine garrison held Bethlehem. His thoughts went back to the past as he dwelt on never to be forgotten memories. His desires were natural as he craved for his old life, but this was neither spiritual; nor helpful to him, to others or to the cause of God. Such longing is never quenched by gratifying the desire, but by replacing it with godly goals.

Under his breath, David sighed, 'Oh, that someone would give me a drink of the water from the well of Bethlehem, which is by the gate!' Hearing this, three of David's mighty men broke through the gate and the Philistine garrison, took some water and brought it to David.

The actions that followed from David's natural desires were spiritual. He was overwhelmed with gratitude, but he shrank from a selfish use of the water. It seemed to him that the water was dyed with the blood of men. After all, God only has the right to receive that for which men have risked their lives. So he resolved to sacrifice the longed-for water to the Lord. He offered to the Lord what was too precious for his own use, and as he did, the water became more precious (see also the woman with the alabaster box of ointment which was poured over Jesus' feet in Mt. 26:6–13). The water of Bethlehem became sweeter to David as he poured it out, than if he had greedily gulped it down.

From these spiritual actions, born from David's natural desires, we can draw a scriptural principle. After all, Abraham was willing to sacrifice his own son Isaac to God. Moses chose to be ill-treated along with the people of God rather than enjoy the pleasures of sin for a short time. David said he would not 'offer burnt offerings to the LORD my God with that which costs me nothing' (2 Sam. 24:24). The psalmist said, 'I will not enter my house or go to my bed – I will allow no sleep to my eyes, no slumber to my eyelids, till I find a place for the Lord, a dwelling for the Mighty One of Jacob' (Ps.132:3–5, NIV). Jesus said, 'He who loves father or mother more than Me is not worthy of Me. And he who loves son or daughter more than Me is not worthy of Me. And he who does not take his cross and follow after Me is not worthy of Me' (Mt. 10:37,38), and 'He who loves his life will lose it, and he who hates his life in this world will keep it for eternal life' (Jn. 12:25). We are urged, 'Therefore, let us go forth to Him, outside the camp, bearing His reproach' (Heb. 13:13). In Revelation 12:11 we read, 'And they overcame [the devil] by the blood of the Lamb and by the word of their testimony, and they did not love their lives to the death.'

## A prosperity gospel

A Christianity which costs nothing, accomplishes nothing. As a Christian I believe, and I belong, but do I obey what the Lord who bought me asks of me? I have only one life, and I want to give it to what the Lord uniquely has for me. So the sacrifice for each person will be different. Therefore, all I have is to be used for His glory. As Amy Carmichael said, 'Nothing is too precious for Jesus.' As the Lord poured out His life for me, surely I should give all to Him.

Just a few miles from my home is the village of Arthington where a century ago millionaire Richard Arthington lived. He was a Cambridge graduate who loved the Lord. He gave his fortune to Baptist missions on the condition that it was used in pioneer evangelism within twenty-five years. He lived in a single room, cooked his own meals and sought to live frugally for the Lord's sake. He wrote, 'Gladly would I make the floor my bed, a box my chair, and another box my table, rather than that men should perish for want of the knowledge of Christ.' Such an attitude is not often found in our evangelical world today. Strangely, we are all rather drawn to a prosperity gospel!

I believe in Jesus; I belong to Jesus, but do I obey Jesus? Has my Christianity sacrificed sacrifice?

# Keep on keeping on

When Pompeii was destroyed by the eruption of Mount Vesuvius, there were many people buried in the ruins. Some were found in cellars, probably having gone there for security. Some were found in the upper rooms of buildings. However, there was one Roman sentinel found standing at the city gate where his captain had placed him, with his hands still grasping his weapon. While the earth shook beneath him, and floods of ashes and cinders covered him, he had stood at his post. And there, in excavations a thousand years later, this faithful man was to be found.

Neatly tucked into the great chapter of faith, Hebrews 11 (v. 27) is a two-word epitaph/biography of one of the great characters of the Old Testament. Describing Moses various translations read, 'He endured' (NKJV), or 'He kept right on' (*The Message*), or He 'held staunchly to his purpose' (AMP). In the book of Hebrews, three others are described as having endured: Abraham (6:15), Hebrew Christians (10:35,36) and Christ (12:3). However, the actual Greek word for 'endured' is only used once in the Bible (Heb. 11:27) and it gives the idea of being strong and firm.

## Starting, finishing and enduring

It is a great thing to start well. It is no small matter to finish strong. However, it is very hard to endure when the going is mundane, dreary or repetitive. My wife teases me concerning the unused diet foods and health books which I once started, but now only clutter our kitchen cupboards. She calls them one of my 'enthusiasms'. Fine beginnings and noble resolutions are not the sole ingredients of endurance. As Jesus pointed out, it is not the start of building the tower, but the ability to continue which counts. One of the hardest things about life is that it is daily. It is hard to express the deep disappointment with those that once ran well but for some reason have ceased to endure. It was not the Lord who moved from them, but they turned from the God of all grace, despite the fact that He gives adequate strength to endure. For me, one of the great evidences of the truth of the gospel is that, forty years after having trusted Christ, I am still as convinced and passionate about it as ever I was. God is well able to keep us. My relationship with God is not one of my passing enthusiasms.

Endurance for Moses was not straightforward. There was a constant barrage of reasons to give up. He was treated with contempt by the world's most powerful man, Pharaoh. The Hebrew people were stubborn, constantly grumbling, blaming Moses, complaining and rebelling. Miriam and Aaron's criticism created words which cut deeply into Moses' heart. There were bitter disappointments, such as when ten of the twelve spies, and then the people of Korah, Dathan and Abiram, led a cold, sinister, sneaky conspiracy against him. These were not the troubles of youth – remember Moses began his greatest work at the age of eighty!

We are told why Moses endured. It was because of 'seeing Him who is invisible' (Heb. 11:27). This was not a once-for-all experience, but for Moses it meant continually keeping the Lord at the centre, a constant drinking at the fountain of God's love and maintaining a sense of eternal purpose. 'Seeing Him' is to be our constant occupation. To keep Christ and eternity not only in view, but also in focus, motivates consistency in our walk with God. Oswald Chambers said, 'We are uncertain of the next step, but we are certain of God. Immediately we abandon ourselves to God, and do the duty that lies nearest, He packs our life with surprises all the time.' Let us keep looking up, for God is continually looking down at us.


**Erosion?**

The greatest danger for those of us who have been on the Christian pathway for some time is that of gentle erosion. There is an initial excitement and enthusiasm about knowing and serving the Lord. However, with the passing of time, there can be slow and steady compromise, which leaves us less and less confident in Christian service. We find it hard to speak up for the Lord when we are not walking with Him. To be relevant we need to be meeting people whose lifestyles may be offensive to us. To be with these people and not get contaminated challenges us to be very close to God. We need to know the world, to know the Word and to know how to communicate the Word to the world.

Moses was not an isolationist. The enduring of Moses included involvements with, leading of, ministering to and lifting up of the people. Effective, enduring ministry is based upon our close relationship with God. Noah built his ark and pleaded with the people for one hundred and twenty years without apparent success. He endured. Jeremiah preached for over sixty years with no positive response to his message. He endured.

Daniel prayed three times a day and found himself in a den of lions. He endured. Isaiah volunteered for service saying, 'Here am I, send me.' Eventually he was sawn in two; but he had endured to the end.

John the Baptist fearlessly spoke the truth to Herod and was beheaded. Again, he had endured.

Peter preached the gospel to Gentiles and others but, according to legend, was crucified upside down. He, too, had endured.

John preached and planted churches, outliving each of the other disciples, and was imprisoned on the Isle of Patmos, but he endured.

Paul suffered for the cause of Christ for over three decades, and was probably burned to death in one of Nero's gardens. He endured, fighting a good fight, and finishing his course.

The Lord Jesus endured both a life of obedience and death by crucifixion. He set the standard, but more. He gives the grace to endure.

Michelangelo said, 'Art is a jealous god. It requires the complete and whole man.' The true and living God makes no less demands, but abundantly blesses us as we go His way. Are we enduring? It is no light question. What really matters as we slide along this new century is endurance. That is the vital barometer of our true commitment. 'Having done all, [let us] stand' (Eph. 6:13). In times of moral and spiritual laxity let us endure. When wickedness appears to be winning let us endure. When in times of crisis let us endure. When no one will know if we have compromised let us endure.

Samuel Zwemer, 'the Apostle to Islam', could say

> I have spent sixty years thinking of the Muslim world and its problems. It began when I signed a card in 1886, expressing my interest in becoming a foreign missionary. Little did I realise all the way God would lead me into Arabia and Egypt and across the world of Islam. We

must not lose faith or courage, but be earnest and stead-fast and diligent until the going down of our Sun – or the rising of His Sun at His glorious appearing. I am here because my Commander-in-chief sent me and I have to stay until His command is rescinded.

Let us endure in our walk with God, our turning away from sin, our habitual prayerfulness, and seeking after holiness. If Christ endured, should not we too? He will be faithful to us . . . always. Can you think of a more commendable epitaph than 'he (or she) endured'? Let it be said of you and me – that we endured.

# The humble poor believe

I want to share some verses that are packed with irony. Soak in the impact of what is being said:

> Now in the fifteenth year of the reign of Tiberius Caesar, Pontius Pilate being governor of Judea, Herod being tetrarch of Galilee, his brother Philip tetrarch of Iturea and the region of Trachonitis, and Lysanias tetrarch of Abilene, while Annas and Caiaphas were high priests, the word of God came to John . . . in the wilderness. (Lk. 3:1–3)

Society was well aware of the political leaders, the royals and the religious figureheads, but the Lord revealed Himself not to them, but to John. And where was he? Not in a presidential estate, palace or temple but in the wilderness. John was not the type whose statue would have been put up in the park, nor whose name hit the headlines, but he did meet with the Creator of the universe, the Lord of all. He was to receive the Word of God that he might then proclaim it to others. And he did that in the wilderness!

## The widow's mite

Religious leaders did not notice her; their hopes for substantial funds were not focused on her, nor were her contributions the type that were regarded as great answers to prayer. Whereas others were conspicuously giving out of their abundance, a widow sacrificially gave just two mites. However, it was this giver whom Jesus noticed and commended. She gave her livelihood, but her sacrifice has never been forgotten.

Mighty Elijah confronted the wicked King Ahab and then was commanded to flee and hide, not by a roaring river, but by the trickling brook Cherith. That soon dried up, but a widow was to sustain him. She was earning her livelihood merely by picking sticks. This was hardly a secure situation on which Elijah could rely. However, she was the one the Lord had prepared for Elijah.

Nehemiah 7 is just one of the many lengthy lists of names in the Bible. We often find them tedious reading, but they teach us that God does not overlook one single person who has sought to faithfully trust and serve Him. Nehemiah even lists the gatekeepers and the sons of Solomon's servants.

At the end of Romans, Paul mentions some of his special friends. Of most of them we know very little. Who knows about Mary (v. 6), or Andronicus and Junia (v. 7), Urbanus and Stachys (v. 9), or Tryphena and Tryphosa (v. 12)? And what about 'Quartus, a brother' (v. 23)? He did not even have a name, just a number; probably he was a slave. Each was special to Paul, and precious to God. Paul never boasts about the national leaders and kings whom he met and preached to. He valued *each* individual, especially his brothers and sisters in Christ.

## God's ways are not our ways

Have you ever wondered why Jesus instructed us as to who we should invite to a feast? 'When you give a dinner or a supper, do not ask your friends, your brothers, your relatives, nor rich neighbours, lest they also invite you back, and you be repaid. But when you give a feast, invite the poor, the maimed, the lame, the blind. And you will be blessed, because they cannot repay you; for you shall be repaid at the resurrection of the just' (Lk. 14:12–14). It is practical teaching that is simply mirroring the example of the Lord Himself. Jesus invites the waifs and strays of society – sinners – to be His friends. Jesus has great love and compassion for the poor and over-looked in society, and He wants us to have the same.

I remember seeing in the newspaper the table plan of guests for the state visit of the French President. Of course the Queen was head of the table, around which were seated politicians, entertainers, media moguls and ambas-sadors. No widows or prophets had been invited, nor would they expect to be. They belong to a different king-dom, which is topsy-turvy as far as this world sees things.

Generally speaking, Christians are not honoured by the world. For that matter, neither was Jesus. The apostle Paul spent more nights in prison cells than in swanky hotels. As believers we seek to simply obey God. We don't have the applause of the world. Our opinions are not particu-larly sought after, rather they are often derided. In fact, those who are supposed to speak on our behalf are often an embarrassment to us. However, as far as I am con-cerned, most of the people I admire are ordinary saints whose quiet, consistent lives really are the salt of the earth. Their service to God is not widely acclaimed, but it speaks volumes of their seeking a 'better country'.

## Not many wise, noble or mighty

Queen Victoria thanked God for the letter 'm' in 1 Corinthians 1: 'not *many* wise according to the flesh, not *many* mighty, not *many* noble are called. But God has chosen the foolish things of the world . . .' Praise God for those in a position of power and influence who are saved, but there are not many. However, God who notices a sparrow fall to the ground sees each one of us as very precious in His sight. We are each the apple of His eye. There is no such thing as an insignificant believer. As children of God we are all very favoured people. It is better to be overlooked by the world but dear to the Lord than the other way round. Significance is found not in the attention the media give us, but in an intimate relationship with God. 'Therefore we make it our aim . . . to be . . . pleasing to Him' (2 Cor. 5:9).

Whoever we are, if we belong to the Lord Jesus, we are privileged to be called His sons and daughters. The Word of God can teach us. We can serve the Almighty God and give for His glory. We can be involved in the glorious tide of the spread of the gospel, and one day we will share eternity with Him.

## A gentle reminder

There is a well-known story of a missionary couple returning from Africa to New York to retire. After years of faithful service they had no pension, their health was broken and they were worn out. As it happened, the missionaries sailed home on the same ship as President Teddy Roosevelt who was returning from one of his big-game hunting expeditions. No one paid attention to the missionaries, but a band awaited the ship to greet the President as he arrived home.

The papers were full of the President's arrival, but the missionaries slipped off the ship and found a cheap room in a poor area. The missionaries felt despondent and disgruntled. They brought the matter to the Lord in prayer and received their answer. It seemed to them that the Lord reminded them, 'But you're not home yet.'

# Sometimes God's people do ungodly things

It was a rare moment. Yorkshire Cricket Club had announced that entry to the ground to see the last day of the England versus South Africa test series in August 1998 was free of charge. As a family, we made our way there and watched England win the test and the series. That day was the only one where I saw Hansie Cronje in action. Tragically, he was killed in a plane crash in June 2002, and my heart was heavy. As a Christian, he had borne a very fine testimony that was acknowledged by all. Yet the obituary columns all prefaced his name with the words 'The disgraced Hansie Cronje . . .' At the funeral service, Peter Pollock, the former South African cricketer and national selector said, 'What Hansie did was wrong, but God forgives the repentant sinner. He stood with no excuses. He took his medicine.'

Time and again, secular and Christian newspapers carry the sad news of godly people who do ungodly things. As members of the family of God, it hurts us deeply. These are people who we have loved, felt proud to be associated with, maybe worked and prayed with, and yet . . .

Of course, this is nothing new. The history of humanity is that of marred and scarred privilege. The Garden of Eden was turned into a paradise lost by an act of deliberate defiance. What more could Adam and Eve have wanted after everything they had been given? Still they ignored God's warning and chose a path of rebellion that led to suffering and death.

## The Achilles heel

Greek mythology tells of Achilles, whose mother dipped him in the River Styx believing that its powerful waters would protect him and make him invulnerable to the attacks of enemy arrows. However, she held him by his heel, and though the waters covered every other part of his body, his heel was left unprotected. One day, so the story goes, when he was a man and fighting in a battle, an arrow fired at him fell short, slivered along the ground and pierced his heel. His 'Achilles heel' was his undoing and led to his death.

Satan has a thousand and one ways to attack and penetrate those who appear strong and resilient. The temptation is to commit mutiny against the rule of God in our lives, and history is riddled with people who dared to defy God in this way. So often, our strength is our undoing and becomes our weakness. *Noah* found grace in the eyes of the Lord, and was preserved when the world was flooded and destroyed; but failed to curtail his appetite, drinking the fruit of his own vineyards, and ending in a drunken and possibly immoral stupor. *Abraham*, a man noted for his faith, exhibited a singular lack of faith when he fathered Ishmael, and brought tears to generations of his descendants. So much was invested in *Jacob*, why did he deceive to obtain an earthly blessing? God's providence would have worked things out for him. The meekest man on all the earth, *Moses*, lost his temper and killed an Egyptian soldier, and later through an impetuous act denied himself the pleasure of leading the people of God into the Promised Land.

*Gideon* led an unforgettable victory against the Midianites, but shortly after abused his position and collected gold for himself, which ruined him. *Jephthah* made a rash, foolish, deadly vow. *Samson's* Achilles heel was his love of attractive women. *David* fell into the same trap. As did his son, *Solomon*. So many of the kings went astray in older years as they established friendly contact with wicked leaders of godless nations. *Elijah* allowed self-pity to get the better of him, and *Jeremiah* wanted out of the calling of God because it was just too lonely and costly for him. *Peter* lost his bold courage and denied the Lord not just once, but three times. And we read of *Demas* and *Diotrephes* who each got it wrong when tested.

**Heed the warnings**

Reaching a position of Christian stability, as well as when we are newly converted, we need to heed the warnings of the Bible lest we fall. As someone said, 'We are free to sin, but not to control sin's consequences.' Nevertheless, it is easy to imagine that we will never be found out, or our excuses will defend and acquit us, or that the grace of God will forgive our transgressions as it has so many times before. But sin has to be accounted for. The passing of time or the dimming of our memory does not eradicate sin. No sin is inconsequential.

When Christ died, He paid the penalty of sin not only that we might be forgiven but also to make sinners into saints. God, through His Holy Spirit, makes us new creatures and gives godly desires, but there is a battle going on. Galatians 5:17 tells us 'For the flesh lusts against the Spirit, and the Spirit against the flesh; and these are contrary to one another, so that you do not do the things that you wish.' At the very least, Christians take sin seriously and want to flee from it. Yet we need God's strength and programme for overcoming the world, the flesh and the devil.

As Oswald Chambers said, 'Christ did not come to scathe sin, but to save us from it.' When tempted let us remember that there is an eye that sees everything, an ear that hears all things and a record of all that we do. Let us reckon ourselves dead to sin, and alive to Christ. Let us run from the very appearance of sin, learning not to expect it, excite it or excuse it. Or, as Jude warns, let us not 'change the grace of our God into a licence for immorality' (Jude 1:4, NIV).

## Who is without sin?

Having said all this, which one of us is without sin? How easily we judge people for their faults and excuse our own. How weak, and vulnerable we are; how prone to wander and leave the God we love. How easily our principles start to fade and wither and yet how hard we are on the mistakes of others. Which other army shoots its own people when they are wounded? Yet, as Christians, we can be very unmerciful to our brothers and sisters in Christ.

If we do sin, may we learn to quickly turn back to our loving Heavenly Father? There is a way back to God; 'the word of the Lord came to Jonah the second time . . .' (Jon. 3:1). It is highly likely that the fornicator whom Paul referred to in 1 Corinthians 5 is the man mentioned in 2 Corinthians 2. Interestingly, whoever it was is kept anonymous. This was not a matter to gossip about, but to grieve over. The sin was treated seriously (1 Cor.

5:6,7), then the sorrow over sin was treated sincerely (1 Cor. 5:9–11), and the sinner was to be treated supportively (2 Cor. 2:7,8).

The story is told of an elderly Welsh preacher who fell down the steps of the pulpit after he had preached. The next day all that the villagers seemed to say to him was, 'I heard you fell yesterday.' Eventually, he replied to one of them, 'You've only heard part of the story. I did fall, but I got up again!'

When Peter was restored to Christ, the issue was 'Peter, do you love me?' How glad I am that we have John 21. For if there was only John 20, we would wonder how we could have Acts 2. God saw fit to include Peter's restoration in Scripture, as well as his fall.

Hansie Cronje is in the best of places with his Best Friend, even if the English cricket team and press have not forgiven him. How readily do we embrace those whose words and actions became a disappointment? How quick are we to forgive those who hurt the Lord's name, and us? Warren Wiersbe in his commentary on 2 Corinthians says about chapter 2 that we should confirm our love for a forgiven brother for their own sake (vv. 7, 8), for the Lord's sake (vv. 9,10) and for the church's sake (v. 11).

> There's a way back to God
> From the dark paths of sin;
> There's a door that is open,
> And you may go in;
> At Calvary's cross is where you begin
> When you come as a sinner
> To Jesus.

# Tender mercies

Samuel Chadwick, founder of the Methodist Cliff College, would test whether potential students had understood anything of the grace of God by asking them to read Genesis 3:9. The tone they used when reading the question to Adam, 'Where are you?' revealed how much they had grasped of God's tender mercies.

Every true Christian is deeply indebted to God's saving grace. Time and again the Scriptures revel in the undeserved love of the Lord towards us. We are so thankful that God has not dealt with us according to our sins, but has shown us mercy beyond measure. In heaven, we will have nothing to boast of, but will praise the goodness of God, recognising that He has loved us with an everlasting love. We have been washed from every sin.

Why then, are we so unforgiving, unmerciful, unloving and uncompassionate to our Christian brothers and sisters who fail, fall, drift or grow spiritually weak? What is it in us which delights to hear that others are not quite as orthodox as we are, or that proudly predicts the downfall of others? Why, as one author expressed it, do we 'shoot our wounded'? Love is the foundation stone of our faith, as well as the character quality that most reflects the Saviour. So why do we sometimes fail to exhibit it towards those in the Christian family who need it most?

In the Bible we read of the tender mercy of our God. C.H. Spurgeon wrote of that phrase

> There is an exceeding melody to my ear as well as to my heart in that word 'tender'. 'Mercy' is music, and 'tender mercy' is the most exquisite form of it, especially to a broken heart. To one who is despondent and despairing, this word is life from the dead. A great sinner, much bruised by the lashes of conscience, will bend his ear this way, and cry, 'Let me hear again the dulcet sound of these words, tender mercy.'[13]

## Would we have bothered with. . . ?

I have a deep fear that Christians, who are the recipients of God's mercy, do not receive mercy from their brothers and sisters in the Lord. Would we have bothered with a Jacob who deceived and twisted to further his own ends? God did! Would we have chosen Moses, a murderer, to lead God's people out of Egypt to the Promised Land? God did! Would we have described David, a man guilty of adultery, manslaughter and self-reliance as 'a man after God's own heart'? God did! Would we have re-commissioned a disobedient Jonah who had to be stopped in his tracks by a great fish, and who hated the people to whom he was sent? God did! Would we have given the keys of the kingdom to Peter, who was to curse in his denying all knowledge of Jesus? God did! Would we have described Jephthah, Samson and Rahab as people of faith? God did!

Don't misunderstand: God is the God of truth and righteousness. He hates sin, and must punish all wrong. He is utterly pure, and has never been able to excuse sin. As a loving, heavenly Father, He will chasten His

disobedient children. His love forbids Him from allowing us to pursue a course of folly or sin. It may be that
the Lord will even take the physical life of a disobedient
Christian, but save their soul (1 Cor. 5:5; 11:30).

However, from the Bible we see how reluctant he is to
judge, and how eager to pardon. God does not want to
destroy his own children. He knows that 'a broken
spirit dries the bones' and has no desire for us to have
sorrow upon sorrow. God wants us to have freedom and
joy in our relationship with Him. Lamentations 3:33
could be translated, 'When the Lord punishes, He has no
heart in.' It is hard to imagine a more stubborn, sinful
and hard-hearted group of people than those to whom
Jeremiah had to minister to. Nevertheless, they were
God's people. Time and again the Lord sent Jeremiah
with the words, 'It may be that they will hear and repent
. . .' So why are we so hasty to judge, write off and condemn members of the same spiritual family to which we
belong?

**The bruised reed**

The Lord Jesus worked with people as they were.
Though He was not tolerant of sin, He was compassionate. Isaiah said of Him, 'A bruised reed He will not
break, And smoking flax He will not quench' (Is. 42:3).
He is called 'Wonderful, Counsellor'. What an example
of tenderness He showed to the woman caught in the act
of adultery, to Thomas with his disbelief, to Peter after
his denials and to Martha who was preoccupied with the
unimportant. We are to make a distinction between
those who are wilfully defiant against the Lord and
those who need our compassion and enduring love
(Jude 22).

If we are to be godly in character surely we will reflect the qualities of God, including tender mercy. The truly great spirit is always gentle. The 'servant of the Lord must not quarrel but be gentle to all . . . and patient' (2 Tim. 2:24). When Paul wrote to the Corinthians, he had to deal with the issue of immorality. He was aware that things were going on which were dishonourable, but even so he only wrote his letter 'with many tears'. When things were put right, and the multitude of sins covered, Paul urged the Christians to forgive, comfort and reaffirm their love to the once wayward believer, lest Satan should take advantage of them (2 Cor. 2:3–11).

It is all too easy to see headlines in the Christian press, and hear attitudes expressed, which I am sure are not Christ-like. The world loves scandal and gossip. The Lord Jesus does not. He was sinless but is described as 'the Friend of sinners'. He told the parable of the prodigal son, which includes the older brother who often sadly is a picture of Christians, as well as the Pharisees of old. Vance Havner said, 'Remember that your brother's fall is not a summons to criticism, but a call to prayer . . . Remember, besides, that you saw him when he fell. You do not know how many times he was sorely tempted and did not fall.'

There are many who once walked, worshipped and worked for the Lord with us, but now are no longer with us. I ask myself, do I earnestly love and pray for them? Do I show them anything of the grace, which I so freely receive from the Lord? I fear that I have too much of a horrible spirit in me, but as grace 'well refines my heart', I pray that it will be replaced by compassion, love, gentleness and more understanding.

# Who was the giant: David or Goliath?

I imagine that the Old Testament's most popular character is David. What a great life he led. The story is of an unknown shepherd boy who became Israel's king. It has details of the rugged warrior who wrote such tender psalms; insights into the life of a man of God who had rebellious children, the strong leader but weak at home. They are all facets of a biography which ring true, having the marks of authenticity.

What was the highlight of his life? If history is the judge, then David is most famous for his killing of Goliath. It is the story of the small defeating the great, the weak having victory over the mighty and righteousness conquering evil. As God's cause triumphs over Satan's, it is encouraging to us all.

## The odds were against David

His father, Jesse, was an old man, and David was the youngest of eight sons. He did not appear to be a high-flyer. The prospects for David who simply looked after a few sheep belonging to his father, did not look great. He was a nobody whom nobody – except God – noticed. Even Samuel almost overlooked young David. For him to confront Goliath – an outsize version of Jonah Lomu – was not war, but murder! David did not even have any armoury, and was to face the giant alone.

## Youth was against David

He had no experience or expertise as a soldier. He had not even been entrusted to fight in King Saul's army. All Jesse asked him to do was to take bread, cheese and grain to his brothers who were the real soldiers. David was rightly appalled by the lack of activity, revealing their lack of trust in God. David's question was, how could God's people or Saul's army be so intimidated by an 'uncircumcised Philistine' who dares to 'defy the armies of the living God?' But all his suggestions seemed like naïve enthusiasm.

## His family were against David

Instead of being challenged by David's confidence in the Lord, his brothers were cutting in their anger towards him. His elder brother said, 'Why did you come down here? And with whom have you left those few sheep in the wilderness? I know your pride and the insolence of your heart, for you have come down to see the battle' (1 Sam. 17:28) – not that there was much of a battle to see. Cynicism is idealism gone sour in the face of frustration. Eliab, like other cynics, was only happy in making the world as barren as he had made it for himself. He read wrong motives into David's right actions.

## King Saul was against David

Saul was head and shoulders taller than all other Israelites, but felt he couldn't take on Goliath. He allowed an ungodly leader to taunt him and leave him timid and terrified. His strategy, which did not include God, left him powerless, inactive and frustrated. When

David volunteered to fight with Goliath, Saul insisted that his armour be worn by David, even though it had proved ineffective for Saul himself. Saul was hung up on externals. David couldn't cope with heavy metal! (Incidentally, just because something appears to work for one person or group, does not mean it will help others, even if they do the rounds telling others that this is the way that things should be done.)

However, God was with David. Faith does not blind us to the externals, but enables us to see beyond them, as we draw on God's power to accomplish what is humanly impossible. David turned the giants he was facing over to the Lord. David's philosophy was, 'the battle is the Lord's'. David may not have been bigger than Goliath, but David's God is bigger than any spiritual threat or foe.

## Seeing things differently

Psalm 78:70–72 explains how God overturned the obstacles which David faced

> He also chose David His servant, and took him from the sheepfolds; from following the ewes that had young He brought him, to shepherd Jacob His people, and Israel His inheritance.
>
> So He shepherded them according to the integrity of his heart, and guided them by the skillfulness of his hands.

*The odds were against David*. But that didn't matter. We read (v. 70) that God chose David, and if God was for him, who could be against him? Goliath despised the day of small things, but David did not.
*Youth was against David*. We read (v. 71) that God took

him from tending the sheep. The Lord had prepared and trained David in solitude, for the bigger, public tests, which would soon come. He had faithfully killed a lion and a bear as he protected his sheep. Now David was ready for greater things. This is how God works: 'If you have raced with men on foot and they have worn you out, how can you compete with horses?' (Jer. 12:5, NIV). David used his memory to recall God's past deliverances and this encouraged him for future battles.

*His family were against David.* God brought him to shepherd his people (v. 71). Sometimes, even our closest family members may be unaware of what God is doing in our lives and preparing us to achieve. We are to be obedient to God's heavenly calling, even if we are misunderstood and misinterpreted.

*King Saul was against David.* David was to be the shepherd of the nation, leading with integrity and skill. God used grace and gift combined as material weapons, which were of far greater power than the sword and spear.

What are the giants you and I face? Which giants does the church face? God still refused to use the material armoury of fearful men who refuse to make the Lord and His Word the centrepiece of their strategy. Has God changed his policy of using the things which are weak to confound the things which are mighty? No, God uses the 'Davids' who, burdened by the cause of those who dare to defy the living God, and recognising their own weakness, go at the Lord's command, to accomplish the impossible, using God's means. We do it for all the glory of the Lord.

# Mind your mentors

Penzance High Street is overlooked by the statue of Sir Humphrey Davey, the distinguished nineteenth-century chemist. It was he who devised the Davey Lamp which saved so many miners' lives. He was a Christian man. On one occasion he was asked what was his greatest discovery. His incisive reply was: 'Michael Faraday', the renowned scientist.

Sir Humphrey had found Faraday, an uneducated son of a blacksmith, taking notes at his lectures, and longing to study science. Michael Faraday had a brilliant mind that would one day eclipse even Humphrey Davey's.

It is a great skill to spot ability, or the potential for it. The Lord Jesus chose twelve men with whom He would live, teach and train. Though He spoke to thousands, He did not feel it a waste to impart so much more to a tiny group whose potential on the surface did not appear great. The great commission includes the words '. . . teaching them  . . .'

The apostle Paul followed Jesus' example. Writing his last letter to his young protégé Paul says strengthen yourself, and then provide spiritual nourishment for others (2 Tim. 2:1,2). It is a great thing to guard the message for ourselves, but vital to commit what we understand and know to others. We each need an open heart to the Lord, so we preserve the truth; and open hands to others so we pass on the truth.

Timothy had learned from listening to sermons, studying the Word, conversations with Paul and spending time with him. He had been discipled and mentored, in the school of Christ.

I feel grateful to God for those who have made an impact in my life, by taking time, befriending and imparting their love for the Lord. There are numerous individuals who bothered with me when they needn't have done. Some will hardly be aware of the lasting impression they made, while others stand out because of their long-term commitment to my spiritual growth. There are those who helped when I was young; there are others who still mentor me today, and I am grateful to the Lord and them. I wonder though, are younger Christians today enjoying the same privilege of being discipled? Could it be there are young people crying out for such help, but we are too busy, or blind to respond?

It has often been repeatedly pointed out that 2 Timothy 2:2 ('And the things you have heard me say in the presence of many witnesses entrust to reliable men who will also be qualified to teach others' NIV) contains four generations of Christians: Paul and Timothy, 'reliable [people]' and 'others'. The Universities and Colleges Christian Fellowship have adopted this verse as their motto in their Relay training programme. The Navigators, an inter-church training organisation say they look for 'F.A.T. people', an acronym for Faithful, Available and Teachable people. By looking for and investing in others, we can pass on abiding, biblical principles to a future generation.

Mentoring has become an issue to talk about in Christian circles, but my plea is for action, so that across the nation, more mature believers will take on board the God-given responsibility to have unforgettable input into the lives of younger Christians. This is something in which all of us can be involved. I am convinced that there are many tender believers who long to have a role model and information/teaching on which to build their lives.

Psychologist Abraham Maslow said there are four levels of learning

1. Unconscious incompetence
2. Conscious incompetence
3. Conscious competence
4. Unconscious competence

So how can we take people from the first to the fourth level? There are three vital factors.


## 1. The subject

Our aim is not to make clones. I remember preaching in the Yorkshire Dales one Good Friday. The leader of the meeting was a dear Yorkshire Christian. However, when he prayed, he did so in a Welsh accent! I later learned that he had 'sat under' the ministry of Dr Martyn Lloyd-Jones for three years. Now, I am not blaming Lloyd-Jones, but in teaching and learning we have to distinguish between the essentials and the incidentals. Accents and mannerisms are incidentals!

Neither are we seeking to reinforce our prejudices or bigotry. As has often been said, 'The main thing is that the main thing is to be the main thing.' As mentors we have a responsibility to teach what is biblical, not merely cultural or fashionable. 1 Corinthians 2:2 ('For I resolved to know nothing while I was with you except Jesus Christ and him crucified', NIV) is indelibly written over all that I seek to do.

Nor are we reproducing a commitment to 'our thing'. There are wonderful Christian organisations, denominations and churches, but Christ reigns over all.

Our desire is to bring people to a deep knowledge of Him. Jesus said, 'A student is not above his teacher' (Mt. 10:24, NIV). Christ-likeness is sufficient. Over the years, my thinking as a Christian has developed. Some ideas I have rejected, some refined and most retained. By focusing on Christ and Him crucified, we can guarantee that what we are imparting is unchanging truth.

We need to teach Christians how to love, read, understand and teach the Bible. There must be teaching on

- how to pray and delight in time spent with God;
- how to grow in wisdom and knowledge and understanding;
- how to avoid sinful pitfalls and foolish behaviour;
- how to be a vibrant witness to others radiating the reality of Christ in every scenario of life.

Also, we will want to teach people to think, to question, to learn and to work. In addition to answering their questions, we will want to question their answers so that they know why they believe, as well as what they believe.

## 2. Ourselves

The quality of our lives will either raise or ruin our ability to influence others. The responsibility and right to influence others derives from a close walk with God. Our integrity and desire that the Lord should be glorified in the life of the one who is being mentored is the qualification to be involved in the work. The warning of Matthew 18:6 is a solemn one.

The mentor will consider

- What do I know, and what do I want these people to know?
- What do I feel, and what do I want these people to feel?
- What do I do, and what do I want these people to do?

True teaching cannot be a regurgitation of lessons learned long ago, but must come from the refreshing overflow of the heart. The manna in the wilderness soon became stale; it had to be gathered and used daily. Similarly, we need to give 'fresh manna' to those with whom we meet. Dr Arnold, the acclaimed headmaster of Rugby School, was asked 'Why continue to study for your pupils? You surely have enough to give them?' He replied, 'It is not because I fear I do not have enough to give them, but because I prefer that they should be supplied from a running stream rather than from a stagnant pool.'

Some of the most exciting and fulfilling people we can meet are those older people who have decided not to stop learning. They are still growing. I can think of at least three ways which help us to go on learning.

First, reading good books. Reading the Bible keeps us sound; reading books keeps us interesting. Prof. Verna Wright, who influenced me so greatly, was a voracious reader and could always talk about the books he had been reading that month, as well as the Scripture he had read that day. Then Warren Wiersbe's two books *Walking with the Giants* and *Listening to the Giants* gave me a thirst for the written word. And I began to read all he had written: he mentored me through his writings. Young Christians will start with just one or two choice books. As Sherlock Holmes said, it's a great thing to begin life with a small amount of good books which are your own, but we converse with great minds of decades past as we read.

Secondly, we are to learn to read people. There is so much to learn from everyone. To look and listen to people can teach great wisdom. Isn't one aspect of maturity to learn to see things as other people see them, and especially as God sees them? The book of Proverbs teaches us how God watches and weighs the world. It is true wisdom, and teaches how people are to behave.

Thirdly, let us allow the Lord to read us. The Holy Spirit uses our soaking ourselves in the Word of God to mould us into the people of His making. He draws near in a special way as we commune with or talk about Him. 'Search me, O God, and know my heart; and see if there is any wicked way in me and lead me in the way everlasting' is a prayer which God answers.

The mentor's character is what produces confidence. Young people will not grow if they feel we are 'as hypocritical as the last guy', nor if they feel we are rehashing that which we are supposed to say, but it is not affecting our lives. True learning brings about change, and God uses able teachers whose resources are not merely found in their own abilities, but in God's grace. Teaching which impacts is not only head to head, but heart to heart.

For effective teachers there is no such thing as a small class. To regularly spend time with one or two is of immense and eternal value. By way of illustration, in 1947 Prof. Chandrasekhar of Chicago University scheduled to teach a seminar in astrophysics. For him it involved considerable commuting twice each week, often in very wintry conditions. However, only two students signed up. The professor kept to his commitment. The students, Chen Ning Yang and Tsung-Dao Lee, did their homework. Ten years later in 1957 they both won the Nobel Prize for physics, as did Prof. Chandrasekhar in 1983. Oh, the joy of being able to invest in the lives of others, who will in turn teach others also!

## 3. The students

Everyone who has had the privilege of being with the very young knows the truth of the proverb 'Foolishness is bound up in the heart of a child.' Be that as it may, children do grow into maturity, as they learn to discern between the good and the best. Howard Hendricks of Dallas Theological Seminary said 'One of the greatest fears I have for my students after graduation is not that they will fail, but that they will succeed in doing the wrong things and reach the end of their lives, and discover that this isn't the destination they wanted and it can't fulfil them.'

Portia Nelson has written a piece entitled 'Autobiography in Five Short Chapters'.[14] It reads

> I: I walk down the street. There is a deep hole in the sidewalk. I fall in. I am lost  . . .  I am helpless. It isn't my fault. It takes forever to find a way out.

> II: I walk down the same street. There is a deep hole in the sidewalk. I pretend I don't see it. I fall in again. I can't believe I am in the same place. But it isn't my fault. It still takes a long time to get out.

> III: I walk down the same street. There is a deep hole in the sidewalk. I see it's there. I still fall in. It's a habit. My eyes are open. I know where I am. It is my fault. I get out immediately.

IV: I walk down the same street. There is a deep hole in the sidewalk. I walk around it.

V: I walk down another street.

I urge us to get to know young people and understand the needs and traits of each age group. They are possibly battling in their minds with issues as big as suicide, direction in life, sex and the church.

God's grace means that each individual has tremendous potential. To label someone may be to libel them. To write off people as being too shy or too self-confident, as a troublemaker or a busybody, is to deny God's transforming power. I'm glad people were patient with me because I shudder at the memory of some of the things I said and did. Let us motivate people, but not out of guilt. Encourage students to learn, to be patient, and give them opportunities to serve in a way that will stretch them. The little ditty is true

I hear and I forget;
I see and I remember;
I do and I understand.

We need to spend time with them, even invest our lives in them, by being available, and always welcoming to them. Again, if I may use Verna Wright as an example, I don't know that I have ever known a busier man, but I never felt I was intruding on him (though I am sure I was). Verna would take me home after meetings and chat about the things of God. Before leaving the car, he would always ask me to pray. He invited me for meals in his home, and to accompany him when he was preaching. Verna's car was, in many ways, my Bible College. He taught me the most basic principles after finding me as a new, young, unpredictable but very enthusiastic Christian. Years later, I regard him as one of my best 'buddies' (he loved that word!) and I still miss him immensely. Verna mentored many people like this. The challenge is whether I have passed on to others what he taught me. Interestingly, I loved the formal meetings which I attended, but I appreciated more the times with Verna over a meal table or driving somewhere.

**Practical proposals**

Perhaps we could pray that we would be able to meet regularly with an individual(s) on a regular basis, either in a home, or in a coffee shop, or over a meal, have informal Bible study, or at least chat about the Bible, some prayer and fellowship and accountability. Times together are part of a growing together, as are fun times, and more fallow periods: all are part of building up the young person into a consistent walk with God.

Nationally, I believe we could use a network of mentor ministries to act as a catalyst encouraging discipling/mentoring, so that throughout the UK older Christians are taking seriously the need to set aside time to invest in young lives, not just expecting them to 'do church'. One-to-one or one-to-small group teaching is biblical, and proved, and needs to be worked again. Each of *us* can be involved!

# My feet nearly slipped

Five hundred years before the birth of Christ, Aeschylus wrote: 'How rare, men with character to praise a friend's success without a trace of envy.'

Centuries earlier, God wrote with His own hand: 'You shall not covet . . . anything that is your neighbour's.' Covetousness and envy are at the heart of the breaking of each of the Ten Commandments. When I break one of the first nine, I break this tenth commandment as well.

Envy, the green-eyed monster, is that destructive cancer within the heart of humans that finds pleasure in seeking to destroy the merit and achievements of others. Its only satisfaction comes when the success of other people is soiled and sapped. Although utterly distasteful and shameful it is rare to find anyone genuinely devoid of this obnoxious sin. Alec Motyer, referring to Romans 13:13 says, 'It is likely that few local churches today are greatly bothered by revelling and drunkenness, debauchery and licentiousness; but it is equally likely that many local churches are harbouring quarrelling and jealousy.'

If envy's relations are pride and greed, its children are numerous and include slander, gossip, theft, cruelty, disorder and destruction. Envy leads to hate, but is not as easily dealt with as hatred. Unchecked envy will lead to a remorseful way of life (Prov. 27:4) and ultimately to estrangement from God (Rom. 1:28–32). While firing at others, envy wounds the attacker. Envy led Cain to murder his brother, Abel. It caused Joseph's brothers first to whisper, then scheme and eventually sell their own brother into slavery. Miriam and Aaron undermined the leadership of Moses because of envy. Gnawing away in Haman's heart was envy so he plotted against godly Mordecai. And, of course, it was the envy of the Jews that led to the rejection and betrayal of Jesus into the hands of Pilate for crucifixion. Therefore, we have to treat envy ruthlessly.

Scripture warns against envying the prosperity of the wicked (Ps. 37:1; Prov. 23:17). However deadly that is, envying the people of God for His blessing on them seems to me to be far more sinister. An Indian legend says that a junior devil could not get a man to sin, so the devil himself told him, 'Have you heard that your brother has been made Bishop of Johannesburg?' This led to envy! We each need to ask the Lord to search our heart to remove it far from us. To envy is to demonstrate a lack of love (1 Cor. 13:4), a spirit of worldliness (1 Cor. 3:3) and a sinful nature (Gal. 5:19–21). It is a demonstration that a desire for the glory of God has become displaced by our own craving for honour.

When one church is seeing greater growth than my own am I envious? When one Christian is given a position in ministry, but I am overlooked, am I envious? When someone is praised but I am not mentioned am I envious? When another person is given an opportunity but not me; or when others have greater vision than I, am I envious?

## Some questions

I have to ask myself

- Do I find it is easier to weep when others weep than it is to rejoice when others rejoice?

- Do I look for ways to speak ill of someone because he or she is experiencing the blessing of God on their life?
- Do I refuse to co-operate with someone else's work, simply because it is theirs and not mine?
- Is competitiveness my motivation for Christian service?
- Do I regularly praise God for the ministry of other people, sincerely praying for the Lord's greater blessing on them?
- Am I using my 'principles' as a guise for envy and an excuse for not advancing the work of others?
- Do I pray that the Lord would help me to be rid of all envy (1 Pet. 2:1)?

**So what do I do?**

The Bible makes it clear that as a Christian I am not to envy but rather to rid myself of it (Gal. 5:25,26). So how is envy eradicated?

- By recognising that envy is a problem that we cannot just ignore. Paul feared for the Corinthian Christians that there may be 'jealousy and quarrelling' (1 Cor. 3:3, NIV) among them. This is not a new problem.
- By confessing it to the Lord as sin, and praying for His Spirit of love to fill our minds.
- By recognising that all that I or anyone else has is from the Lord. John the Baptist seeing his followers leave him to follow the Lord Jesus answered and sent a message to us all, 'A man can receive nothing unless it has been given to him from heaven' (Jn. 3:27).
- By putting a guard on our lips so that we do not speak evil of others.

- By praying for God's blessing on specific individuals and so becoming part of their ministry through our prayerful support. When F.B. Meyer first held meetings at Northfield, Massachusetts, large crowds thronged to hear his stirring messages. Then G. Campbell Morgan went to Northfield. The people were soon flocking to hear his brilliant expositions of Scripture. Meyer confessed that at first he was envious. He said, 'The only way I can conquer my feeling is to pray for Morgan – which I do!'
- By praising God for what He is doing in and through other people, especially those whose ministry is similar to our own.
- To specifically do all for the glory of God, giving Him the praise rather than seeking to promote ourselves. Henrietta Mears said: 'The man who keeps busy helping the man below him won't have time to envy the man above him – and there may not be anybody above him anyway.'

Let the Word of God have the final word: 'Since we live by the Spirit, let us keep in step with the Spirit. Let us not become conceited, provoking and envying each other' (Gal. 5:25,26, NIV).

# Lessons from the kings of Judah

Along the front façade of Notre Dame Cathedral in Paris are twenty-eight sculptures of the kings of Judah. Of course, we don't know what their physical appearance was, but 2 Chronicles gives insights as to what they were like on the inside. The books of Chronicles (one book originally) are sermons, based on the factual history of Israel and Judah. The author lets the facts speak, and what they say edifies us. The second book of Chronicles is a great read, and has glaring lessons for the reader to learn. Here are some.

1. *The battle is the Lord's.* The kings who acted on this truth found that God gave them victory; those who forgot the lesson, believing that they could succeed without the aid of God, were reminded, at great cost, of their own inability (see 20:12; 14:11; 18:31; 25:8; 32:8). I have a friend who each morning in his quiet time with the Lord, by faith, puts on the armour of God. As Francis Ridley Havergill wrote: 'each piece, put on with prayer'.

2. *None of the kings of Judah was sinless.* There were some wonderful men among the kings, but all had their faults. Even some of the royal children of godly kings became ungodly themselves. Each king of Judah must have left people longing for the coming of the King of

kings, who would be pure, sinless and undefiled. They all point the way to His royal birth, and His kingly reign. The truth is that all Scripture is about Jesus.

3. *Kings who started well did not necessarily end well.* To my mind the saddest reading in 2 Chronicles is when good and godly kings in their youth, lost their submission to God's ways as they grew older. Some were not able to be trusted with the blessings that God gave (e.g. 26:16). As someone said, 'We are always shaping our future, and reaping our past.' Usually the kings who went astray did so because they made affinity with ungodly monarchs. Putting their confidence in the wrong people was their besetting sin (see 16:3; 18:1–3; 20:35; 21:6; 35:20,21).

4. *When a leader sinned, tragically ordinary people suffered* (25:22; 33:9). There is great responsibility therefore for leaders (whether in a nation, or the church) to live in a godly way, and set an example that is worth being followed. Notice how the nation needed kings, priests and prophets, to enjoy God's blessings, for behind the scenes, Satan is at work.

5. *No matter how wicked a king had been, when there was true repentance there was abundant mercy.* God used affliction to humble wicked Manasseh (33:12). God sees all things, and works when there is humility and a tender heart. This certainly encourages us to pray despite the horrid waywardness of our nation at the moment (12:12; 20:3; 34:27). If Judah is similar to the church, then there is a challenge here to all Christian leaders, and the promise of blessing when there is true repentance.

6. *It was necessary at times to purge the land of accumulated sin*. Time and again the nation of Judah allowed an infiltration of spiritual neglect and idolatry (15:17; 20:33). There had to be a complete purging of all evil from the nation, to enjoy God's blessings again (14:2,3; 17:6). Prosperity in the land came through seeking the Lord (26:5; 31:10). The nation demonstrated the New Testament truth that you reap what you sow (see also 21:20). Five times revival came during the reign of the godly kings Asa, Jehoshaphat, Joash, Hezekiah and Josiah.

7. *Even in times when most prophets were apostates, there were some who fearlessly and faithfully spoke the Word of God, whatever the cost*. The monarchs, the prophets, the priests and the people, had to discern whether what was being proclaimed was indeed the Word of God rather than the dreams and thoughts of mere men (15:1–3; 18:13,26,27; 20:37).

The value of 2 Chronicles is that God wants to foster a right relationship between Himself and His people through the sermon based on real history. Through the recording of this period of history, there is a selection of events, and then a proclamation of the pattern of failure and judgement, as well as grace and restoration.

# Vote with the cross

During my years in the sixth form, the desk in front of me was occupied by Jon, a seventeen-year-old Trotskyite. He was enthusiastic . . . but then so was I! We studied the same subjects, came from similar backgrounds, but were as different as chalk from cheese when it came to the things of God. We frequently discussed spiritual issues. On occasions he even came and listened to the open-air meetings in which I was involved in the centre of Leeds twice a week. Eventually he became the leader of Leeds City Council and now holds one of Labour's safest seats as MP (I suspect his views have been moderated somewhat, but then perhaps mine have as well!).

Politics has been called 'the art of the possible'. Politicians react to situations. Month by month we are bombarded with political intrigue from both sides of the Atlantic. Although I am aware that we all have our own personal views, I am convinced that politicians cannot meet the real needs of men and women. In fact, I fear that politics is usually a distraction from the pressing necessity to make known the gospel of Jesus Christ. God's agenda for these times is very different from that of the media or parliament. They are frequently asking the wrong questions and therefore receiving the wrong answers. As Christians we have a relationship with the God of the impossible. He works to further His ultimate plan for us. God has written the agenda for this world which He created. No politician or ideology can possibly interfere with what God has in store for us.

However, don't misunderstand. We do need government and therefore politicians. As Oswald Chambers said, 'There is a complication of forces to be dealt with which most of us know nothing about. We have no affinity for this kind of thing, and it is easy to ignore the condition of the men who have to live there, and to pass condemnation on them.' The Bible teaches that the state has authority and 'the authorities that exist are appointed by God' (Rom. 13:1). Rulers are 'God's minister[s]' and we are to 'be subject' to them (Rom. 13:4,5). There are occasions when the church and state clash. In this situation believers are to obey God rather than humans. We are to pray for those who lead us and to use the freedom of our democratic systems to influence them for good. However, neither parliament nor the judiciary will usher in a Christian country. In fact, despite extensive lobbying from Christian groups, sadly much recent legislation has been directly opposed to the Ten Commandments.

Often Christianity has thrived in the most ungodly regimes. The Roman Empire was far from welcoming towards Christianity, but we do not read of Jesus, Paul, Peter, John or James using their energy to pronounce against Caesar or the military regime. On the contrary, 'Render . . . to Caesar the things that are Caesar's, and to God the things that are God's' (Mt. 22:21) is the Lord's instruction. Even the awful human abuse of slavery was not the priority of the early Christians. Christ was their consuming passion and the gospel was their message. Souls needed to be saved and the church gave itself to this supreme task. In our secular age, dare we do less? I have no doubt that if multitudes are converted, there will be social and political by-products. Who knows?

God may raise up another William Wilberforce or Lord Shaftesbury. Politicians would have to react to the Christian consensus, but for the moment, in the West, Christians are in the minority.


## Why this article?

I am aware that US President Calvin Coolidge, a man of few words, said, 'I found out early in life that you never have to explain something that you haven't said.' So why am I writing this article?

Because I am concerned that, in following the daily news, we may be forgetful that we are primarily citizens of heaven, and servants of God. We are ambassadors, representing to those we know, a greater kingdom. Nothing can exaggerate the urgency of evangelism. We are to implore people to be reconciled to God. Political issues, important as they are, fade into insignificance compared with the eternal destiny of men and women. Current affairs can be as much an addictive idol as the love of money, or a time-consuming hobby.

I am concerned that the focus of our attention and confidence can be subtly set on other human beings and not on the Lord. It is He alone who can truly change the hearts of men and women.

Could it be that in the media-generated excitement over political tides and elections, our imagination is captured by issues that do not bless the heart as would a consistent walk with God?

**Some questions**

❑ Is the first part of my day spent listening to the latest news or meeting with God?

❑ Do I spend more time with my newspaper(s) than my Bible?

❑ Have I become more concerned about whether my country goes left or right, than whether people are going to heaven or hell?

❑ Have I been deceived into believing that a party or politician can bring what in reality only Christ can bring to this earth?

❑ Could I be alienating people, who are either brothers or sisters in Christ, or lost souls who need to be saved, by my strident political views?

❑ Do my friends know more of my politics than of my Christ?

❑ Do I pray for those who rule our land?

❑ When it comes to my citizenship on earth and in heaven, do I have my priorities right?

From time to time I pray for my old school friend, Jon. I wonder if he will ever be converted? I don't know how many Christian MPs put biblical principles before party demands, but it would be good if he were to become one. Let us each strive to put our trust in the Lord rather than kings or rulers.

# Marriage – God's blueprint

It is a joy to congratulate a newly married couple. The sense of anticipation and excitement as two lovers start their lives as a couple is tangible. Let us pray for those in our churches who are starting out on married life. As student leader, Nigel Pollock said

> Weddings are places where you encounter the students of yesterday and get some sense of the people they are becoming. Are they standing for the gospel, integrating faith and work, concerned for God's world, serving in their local church, using their resources to practice hospitality and resource mission or can you see the signs of compromise, greed, self-centredness and pride?

## God thought of it

Marriage is a foundation principle of the Bible. At the beginning of time, God instructed 'Therefore a man shall leave his father and mother and be joined to his wife, and they shall become one flesh.' What we read in Genesis 2:24 is repeated by the Lord Jesus and the apostle Paul.

First, God designed us, and then He designed marriage, and all that comes from God for us is very good. Marriage involves leaving and cleaving. God instructs those who marry to leave their parents and cleave to their spouse. Leaving doesn't mean that we have to abandon or utterly forsake our parents, especially as they grow older! It does mean a moving on to a new commitment, and a submission to a new authority. The gift of marriage is so precious it is remarkable that all too often marriage can be the entrance to disaster. William Wordsworth expressed the same bewilderment when he wrote

> Why do not words, and kiss, and solemn pledge;
> And nature that is kind in woman's breast,
> And reason that is in man is wise and good,
> And fear of Him who is a righteous Judge,
> Why do not these prevail for human life,
> To keep two hearts together, that began
> Their spring-time with one love . . .[15]

Marriage is a gift from God, and

## We enjoy the benefits of it

The Bible says in Proverbs 18:22: 'He who finds a wife, finds a good thing and obtains favour from the Lord.' Martin Luther, writing about five hundred years ago said, 'There is no more lovely, friendly or charming relationship, communion or company than a good marriage.'

However, successful marriage demands a divorce, but it is a divorce from our own self-love. Married people have to learn to put their spouse first. But what a privilege to live in a relationship with someone who loves God and loves their spouse, and is committed to their well-being. Imagine two rivers flowing smoothly and quietly until they meet and join into one river. Suddenly the rivers clash and hurl themselves at one another, until gradually there is a newly formed, broad, majestic river which begins to flow downstream as it quietens down and flows smoothly and powerfully. Marriage can be like that.

One of the finest sermons I have ever heard, preached over twenty years ago, was by a black American, E.V. Hill. I read a few years ago that he lost his wife, Jane, to cancer. At her funeral he described the ways this 'classy lady' made him a better man.

When financially struggling, he invested money in buying a petrol station. His wife urged him not to, but ignoring her, he went ahead. He lost all his investment. When he phoned to tell her, she didn't say, 'I told you so', but 'All right.' Later she said, 'As you don't drink or smoke, I reckon we have saved a load of money, so it balances out!'

One night he came home, and there was a candlelit dinner for two. It was only later, when he went to the bathroom, and there was no light, that he realised that there was no money to pay the electricity bill. Even though she had been brought up in a well-to-do home, she never grumbled, but made the best of a difficult situation. Clearly she had learned the lesson that blessing comes in marriage when you put yourself last.


## We neglect it at our peril

God's pattern for society, and for us, is that marriage and family life is to be the fabric of its structure. Society may prefer to 'live together', but such a relationship is not sanctioned by God. God, who knows best, commanded and commended the public coming together of one man and one woman in a legal, lifetime commitment. Despite bulges, baldness, bunions and bifocals, and whether one loses health and wealth, looks and charm, there is to be faithfulness. There is a forsaking of all others, and a loyal, faithful joining to the spouse. This excludes all extra-marital affairs and any shadow of unfaithfulness.

Of course, there are those who for one reason or another, are to remain single. Their role in society and church cannot be overstated, and it may be that they will play a particularly significant part in the work of God, which if they were to be 'distracted' by marriage they could not fulfil to the same extent.

For those who are married, there is the abiding challenge not to neglect the commitment to one's partner. This has to be worked at. We are all aware how easily things can go wrong. Like everything else, it takes time and effort to make a successful marriage, but it is worth it. God is the witness to every marriage ceremony, and will be the witness to every violation of its vows.

Marriage partners need to be good lovers and good forgivers. The phrases, 'I love you' and 'I am sorry' are those which keep a marriage vibrant and full of delight. Pride, selfishness, bitterness, ingratitude, stubbornness, impatience and harshness are enemies of a good marriage.

A grandmother, celebrating her golden wedding anniversary, told the secret of her long and happy marriage. 'On my wedding day, I decided to make a list of ten of my husband's faults, which, for the sake of our marriage, I would overlook,' she said.

When asked what some of the faults were she replied, 'To tell you the truth, I never did get around to listing them. But whenever my husband did something that made me hopping mad, I would say to myself, *Lucky for him that's one of the ten*.'

**And it pictures something even more wonderful**

Sadly, not all marriages work. Difficulty and divorce are all too common. But even successful marriages eventually end, as we are reminded in the wedding service with the words "til death us do part'.

Throughout the Bible, God uses the marriage relationship as a picture of the relationship, which He has with His people. Marriage is about two people, who were previously strangers, being drawn together, into a relationship of mutual, sacrificial love. They become the best of friends.

What a precious picture of what God has done for us: we who were once alienated from Him by our sin, have been drawn to Him by His grace. This is the greatest expression of love the world has ever seen – the Father sent the Son (Jesus) to be the Saviour of the world. This love took Jesus to the cross . . . and the tomb. Jesus bore our sins in His body on the cross of Calvary. He died to buy and bring us into a relationship with Himself that is eternal and loving.

Important as marriage is, it does not involve *the* most important decision. Far more crucial is the establishment of a relationship with Almighty God. This can only be done through Jesus Christ. And, once a person truly repents and trusts Christ, he or she enters into an intimate relationship with God, which grows and goes on forever. Everyone who comes to know God finds in Him a Friend who is loving, forgiving and faithful at all times.

# Exams – a testing time

In parts of Africa they cut flesh and rub dye into the wounds. On Pacific islands, they used to put youngsters through fire and watch their endurance of excruciating pain and fearful anguish. Today, we ask teens to learn by heart hundreds of soon-to-be-forgotten facts, and then isolate them in a hall with many others in an endurance test that will last hours, and has been dreaded for years. Examinations are today's initiation ceremony. Everyone who has experienced the agony of the constant pressure to revise and perform well, longs for the day when the final test has been put behind them.

It is normal to ask, 'Is it worth it all?' Many start to ask themselves whether they could be earning more without qualifications. When they are really feeling low, they wonder whether their parents and teachers are involved in a conspiracy to make sure they don't enjoy their youth. After all, they have many other more interesting commitments, so why waste time on exams? I used to wonder why it is that exams always seem to coincide with the warmest seasons of the year, especially as deep down we all know that one can't revise when sitting in a deckchair, sunbathing and thoroughly distracted.

I remember a doctor explaining how he divided his university course into three stages. The first lasted for years – the period of oblivious optimism. This changed six weeks before his finals into profound pessimism! As he went into the exam room he was in the final stage of frozen fatalism.

However, there are benefits from exams which we can lock into and then make the most of this gruelling period of life. Don't misunderstand, I'm glad exams are behind me, but if you are a Christian, here are ten blessings to be derived from exams:

1. The Bible says: 'It is good for a man to bear the yoke while he is young' (Lam. 3:27, NIV). The Lord understands every phase of our lives. He notices people who are faithful in little things, and later entrusts greater responsibilities to them.

2. Exams teach self-discipline and orderliness. Hudson Taylor, the great pioneer missionary, said, 'A person may be dedicated and devoted, but if ill-disciplined, useless.' To learn discipline is one of life's greatest lessons, and if not learned in youth, it will probably never be learned at all. Get into the habit of making definite plans, which are then prioritised and kept to.

3. Exams teach us that everything that is worth having is to be worked for. The person who has everything handed to him or her on a plate is frustrated, unhappy and spoilt.

4. Exams teach the principle of setting aside immediate pleasure for the sake of something better yet to come. Deferred gratification is not just a principle for our society, but of Scripture itself. Whatever you may have to endure now is nothing

compared with the glory you will enjoy in eternity and for eternity.

The Lord has given us six days to work and a day of rest and worship. I particularly enjoyed the Lord's Day as a student, with its provision for total rest from revision without the nagging voice of conscience reminding me to work. If I didn't work on other days, I felt guilty, but not on Sunday!

The rest and relaxation after the exams are over is all the more enjoyable if one has sought to do one's best beforehand. Relaxation without guilt is a blessing experienced by those who know that they have given their best.

5. Exams give the Christian the opportunity to prove the reality of prayer and faith, as we learn to commit our ways and our work to the Lord. Pray regarding your revision and the examinations themselves. Prove the Lord's willingness to answer prayer, while involved in this phase of your life.

6. Exams give the Christian student the opportunity to glorify God while doing the mundane and boring. Ask God to help you to glorify Him (bring honour to His name) as you sit and slog at your desk. (Notice 1 Cor. 10:31; 6:20.)

7. Exams give the Christian the opportunity to witness to fellow students by showing the peace which God gives in the face of examinations, whatever you believe the results might be (Col. 3:1)! A confident belief in the Lord and Psalm 18:30 ('As for God, His way is perfect') is in itself convincing evidence of your Christian testimony.

8. Exams are a reminder of human weakness and frailty! In this day of proud self-sufficiency that is a valuable lesson to keep in mind.

9. Exams are an apt reminder of the fact that a testing day – the Day of Judgement – is yet to come!

10. At the time of the results, exams give opportunity to either give glory to God, or cast your burden upon the Lord.

Christians are doubly the Lord's. We are His by right because He made us; we are His by redemption because He bought us with His own blood.

We are to be sanctified for the Master's use, and whatever the final outcome, spend time with God and ask Him what is to be your next step. Put God first in all things.

God has often used results different to the ones people expected, to direct and lead them into service better than they expected. Disappointment can be God's appointment. Remember, no matter how you do, God does not fail (Zeph. 3:5), and can be trusted and thanked in all circumstances.

# Section 3

# Our relationship with the lost

When I was younger, we used to sing a song which included the line about every person in every nation in every succeeding generation having the right to hear the news that Jesus Christ can save. How true! Could anything be sadder than to go through life without anyone ever praying for you, or telling you the good news of Jesus and His love, and warning of the serious plight of being outside Christ?

There is such joy to be found in leading people to Jesus that, from a selfish point of view alone, we need to speak and share the gospel. This is not only the task of evangelists, but every Christian should desire to witness to others. To turn small talk into big talk, inconsequential chatter into conversation about the most significant issue of all, is part of our life's work. I long to see all our churches becoming evangelising centres, where it is evident to all around that God is at work through that particular church. And I long to see each individual Christian involved in the ongoing work of witnessing about Jesus to as many as possible.

This group of articles is aimed to stir us up, and help equip us for the task to which every Christian is called.

# The Thinker

In 1880 Auguste Rodin, an unbeliever, presented his famous sculpture 'The Thinker'. It is not depicting an introspective philosopher, but rather portrays a man pondering the plight of men and women who are in hell, a thought that haunted Rodin's imagination. Hudson Taylor, on his return from China to England, endured sleepless nights at the thought of a million Chinese every month going to hell. The apostle Paul said, '. . . I have great sorrow and continual grief in my heart. For I could wish that I myself were accursed from Christ for my brethren, my countrymen . . . my heart's desire and prayer to God for Israel is that they may be saved' (Rom. 9:2,3; 10:1).

Jesus' coming to earth, His death on the cross and resurrection from the dead was so that He might be Lord (Rom. 14:9). However, His compassion for the lost was such that He felt the burden of men and women who are without God and hope in this world and eternity. Picture Him weeping over Jerusalem, or grieving about the wrong decision of the rich young ruler, or commissioning the disciples to preach the gospel to every creature. He loved people, and wanted them to be set on a course whereby they were right with God in life and throughout eternity. We read that, 'for the joy that was set before Him, [He] endured the cross' (Heb. 12:2). That joy must have included the knowledge that many would pass from Satan's domain into the kingdom of heaven. There would be millions who would enjoy eternal fellowship with Him because of the break in fellowship between Him and His Father, which he endured as He hung on the cross.

To preach about hell needs great gentleness and compassion. I cringe when I hear people threatening hell to those who appear disinterested. Tears should be in our hearts, if not our eyes, whenever we mention hell in our presentation of the gospel. We are not to be harsh, but gentle. I fear, though, that the Christian world has blinkered itself to the sight of hell, stopped its ears to the cries of the lost and hardened its heart to the plight of people outside God's grace. This has many consequences, but let me mention three.

## Our preaching

The heartbeat of true gospel preaching will be the glory of God and the needs of the lost. The greatest 'right' that people have is to hear the news that Christ died for their sin. Jonathan Edwards, the eighteenth-century American philosopher/theologian wrote the famous and stirring sermon, 'Sinners in the hands of an angry God'.[16] The style of the message may not be appropriate today, but the truth of the doctrine preached has not changed. To plead with men and women to repent and believe the gospel is the natural outcome of having a glimpse of the plight of the lost.

If a firefighter risks his life to save an individual trapped in a burning building; if a helicopter pilot hazards all to rescue a fisherman from the storms at sea, or a soldier endures unmitigated hardship to defend his country's borders, why do I find it so unpalatable to sacrifice all to save some from God's righteous wrath?

My heart is set free by the grace of God, but it is also burdened for the eternal needs of people around me. I want my gospel preaching to be immersed in the compassion of Christ to such an extent that I have to proclaim the need to repent, and warn of judgement and hell. I cannot omit unpalatable truths because I fear people will not listen. Not to mention sin, judgement or hell may be politically correct and endearing to the crowds, but it reveals lack of tenderness in my heart, and a reliance on my abilities rather than the Holy Spirit to use my proclamation to bring people to saving faith. It is neither honest nor safe to put to one side the consequences of those who are without Christ.

## Our praying

Abraham prayed fervently for Sodom, and Moses for the Israelites; Samuel prayed for the kings, and Nehemiah and Jeremiah for their nation. Jesus prayed for His executioners, and Stephen for his murderers; Paul prayed for the unsaved and urged us to pray for all men and women. Of course, we are commanded to pray, but even if there were no such commands, surely our experience of the love of Christ would constrain us to pray for those who never pray for themselves.

You and I are constantly rubbing shoulders with people who are headed to eternity without being reconciled to God. We will speak to as many as possible, but we can pray for many more. Who knows, you and I may be the only person who will ever pray for them. We can ask the Lord to work in their hearts and save them. We can plead with the God of mercy to be merciful to them.

**Our priorities**

Praying changes our priorities. There is a crying need for us to get out of our comfort zones and be people of action and vision. I am constantly being urged to slow down, but I find it hard to do so when the relentless movement of millions of men and women is towards hell. I know that saving people is God's great work, but I want to give all that God has given me to reach men, women and children with the gospel. Surely there are creative ways we can use to reach the lost. Thousands of people worked frenetically to try to save three astronauts when Apollo 13 hit problems. Nothing is too much effort to seek to save souls who have an eternity ahead of them.

Of course, God wants us to enjoy His world, and the people around us; we have our jobs to earn money, but the main reason for our lives is to glorify God in what we are doing. We desire to become more like Jesus; for Him to be Lord of every part of our being; and to reach and win people for Christ. The people we meet, whether in a summer job or long-term employment, are people who need to be saved, and God has sent us there to reach them. Peter and John expressed this attitude well, saying, '. . . we cannot but speak the things which we have seen and heard' (Acts 4:20). Their compulsion was a risky business, but they could not be silenced; they had to speak to people about Christ. The apostle Paul became all things to all men that he might save some. Instead, we too easily pride ourselves in our churches and our reputation. We hold on to all we have made and built. But such pride, preserving the way we do things, kills compassion and creativity – and with it, jeopardises the people we can reach.

I am aware that distributing tracts may not be the most effective means of reaching people, but if that is the best

I can do, let me do it! Long-term witness with family, friends and work colleagues takes time and patience, but let me be involved in their lives that I may introduce them to Christ. Inviting people I know to go through *Christianity Explored* with me may not shake the earth, but it may lead to an eternal change in the hearts of some. Preaching in the open air may not hit the headlines, but it may be a bridge to a few hearts. Quietly, faithfully praying for the work of God in people's lives, in our churches, and in missionary endeavour will never earn the world's accolades, but what a significant work it is, and one that God honours above all else. Faithful personal work may never lead to my statue being erected in the city square, but by God's grace some may spend eternity with the Lord as a result of that work. Inviting and bringing people to church may not ensure that *The Times* write my obituary, but 'those who lead many to righteousness, [shall shine] like the stars for ever and ever' (Dan. 12:3, NIV). My giving may not gain for me a knighthood, but if it leads to the furtherance of the gospel, I will see giving as a privilege. I may not be the cleverest or most able of orators, but I would like to use the breath God gives me to share a message that reflects the cry: 'Behold, behold the Lamb.'

To sum up, the media's agenda is not God's; so let me not be moulded by it. My neighbour's lifestyle is not the one I am commanded to imitate; they do not set the standard for my life. The Lord Jesus does that. And as missionary C.T. Studd said, 'If Jesus Christ be God, and died for me, then no sacrifice I can make is too great for Him.'

Let us learn from Rodin's 'The Thinker'; and may those thoughts turn to action, as we seek in the words of an old hymn, to rescue those who are perishing.

# Any new babies in the family?

'"Stand up Mr Thomas," said Dr Martyn Lloyd-Jones, pastor of Sandfields Church, "and let them see the latest monument to the grace of God." And he stood and joined us, a very "elderly babe" in Christ, but as precious to all the church as any new baby in a natural family.' So wrote Mrs Bethan Lloyd-Jones, in her *Memories of Sandfields*.[17]

Let us also take up his challenge and ask ourselves, and our churches, 'When did I last, through the grace of God, win an individual to Christ?' I am aware of very faithful Christians who have lived consistent Christian lives at work, in their free time and at home and yet have never known anyone be converted through their witness. In those cases, and there are many, the results of their work has to be left to God, who will have done His own work through their faithfulness. Nevertheless, I know that their desire is that they will see people for whom they have prayed being converted.

Does God want our church to be in the centre of evangelistic endeavour? Is it His desire that people should not perish but come to repentance and faith through the Christ? Has He not given us an example, in the book of Acts, of an early church's struggles, prayers, zeal, passion and also great fruitfulness? Then, could it be that something has gone wrong with us? Don't we earnestly pray that God would once again take us and use us greatly in winning men and women for Him?

I hear talk of reaching the 'unchurched'. That is a big task these days. However, our call is to reach the unsaved, and many of those in church are still ignorant of the gospel. As Christian people, and as churches, we have a responsibility to proclaim the gospel to every creature. A few of them are in our churches; others are in 'churches' which are of no spiritual help to them; most of them have little or no knowledge of the things of God. We are under orders to preach the gospel. Our responsibility is to reach this generation, i.e. the globe. The church should be the spearhead of strategic evangelism in society. It should be a centre where souls are saved and then built up in the faith, so that they in turn may be used to reach others. How I long to see an increasing number of churches, and people, who are giving their lives to the supreme task of rescuing the perishing.

**Where are the people?**

In Acts we find the church praying and preaching. The whole Christian community was involved in this though, of course, there were figureheads. What is striking is that Christ was preached where the people were. A friend cynically commented to me, when his church was celebrating its centenary, 'We are commemorating the fact that we have kept the gospel in these four walls for one hundred years.' In Acts the gospel was taken to the streets, the marketplace, the synagogues, debating chambers, from house to house and to ships. Nobody was exempt from hearing the message, whether slave or master, king or peasant. If they were human they had an eternal existence. There was an awareness that all needed to be saved; each had the right to hear the gospel. We need to think where people are, and then without compromising, seek to reach them there. Christians with secular jobs have the very special position of working with people who possibly have little contact with the gospel. They are strategically placed on the front line, and have great privilege and responsibility to share the gospel with their colleagues.

People are still on the streets; they still go to the markets and shopping centres. There are still queues for the cinemas, discos and football matches. People can be reached in their homes; people still read (!); some will be willing to have one-to-one home Bible studies.

Teenagers will drop into open homes other than their own, where they are welcomed and accepted. From such a backcloth some are willing to think through eternal issues and need not be dragged into a sex-crazed drug culture, moulded by celebrities and friends exerting peer pressure on them. Thankfully, not everyone is into this!

Let us not be intimidated into silence in the workplace, outside the school gate, at the sports club, or in our neighbourhood. No one has the right to tell us not to witness. We have something amazing to offer to men and women with all the things we celebrate, compared with the sadness, frustrations, injustice, cruelty and mess which dominate the headlines. Let us go and tell the world of a wonderful God who made the beauty of the world in which we live; that though we have sinned, the Father sent the Son to be the Saviour of the world; that Jesus who died for our sins, rose again, and by His Spirit will live in the lives of those who believe in Him, and of the wonder and joy of knowing Him on earth and in eternity.

Evangelism is not the task of the young people only. Old people also have souls that need rescuing. Christian youth needs role models of older people who are giving their lives to reaching the lost. We are constantly rubbing shoulders with people who are outside Christ and are not even aware that they are lost.

The greatest needs that people have are not the ones the government, media or education system focus on. People around us are going to hell. The situation is desperate. Inroads into the world of the unsaved cannot be left to others. We should all have unconverted friends whom we are trying to lead to Christ. Each church and Christian is to be engaged in a sacrificial mission, seeking to save those who are outside Christ. If we are truly following the Lord, we will want to be fishers of men – not just influencing the fish, but catching them.

Let us encourage each member of our church to be involved in the work of reaching others at home or abroad. As evangelicals we often equate 'commitment' with 'attendance at meetings'. If somebody is involved in Christian committees and part of a church programme, we feel all must be well. But are they involved in proclaiming the gospel to men and women? We are not Christians just doing our own thing, but in fellowship with others we are reaching into their community. It is right that followers of Christ should be regular in attending, and praying at prayer meetings, but should not the same Christians be involved in making and cultivating genuine friends? I believe in separation from all that is wrong in the world, but there must be involvement with the lost or we will become hardened to their eternal needs. As members of churches, let us know and pray for each other's unsaved friends and relatives, so being part of the ongoing personal work of our Christian friends. It is right to be involved in people's lives, so that we are interested in them, rather than just having token friends. It is too easy to live in a Christian bubble and have little concept of the issues that non-Christians face.


**Ten practical suggestions**

1. The church should organise regular evangelistic events, appropriate for the type of people we are aiming to reach, and such that all the Christians feel able to bring along their unconverted friends. People who come are usually people who are brought. In preaching let us jettison the jargon so that the gospel comes across as clear, relevant and simple.

2. Week by week the church prayer meeting could include a time when all are encouraged to share for prayer those they have witnessed to recently or will be meeting soon.

3. The church should have a prayerful, carefully thought out strategy of evangelism, which involves as many as possible in various types of evangelism, so that all sections of the community are systematically reached. It should be expected that each church member is involved in this to some extent. By using young people in the open air, old folks' homes, school Christian Unions etc., they can be encouraged to begin speaking publicly. Passion for souls is usually caught rather than taught.

4. From time to time there could be special evangelistic endeavours which will be a focus of prayer, work and follow up. Children's and adult missions can be very fruitful. Call in someone with special evangelistic gifts to help you.

5. Pray for 'open homes' where all and sundry can pop in at any time to find a warm welcome and the opportunity to speak of the Lord. Effective youth work needs this as an almost basic necessity.

6. Let us encourage a spirit of expectancy. We can pray for people to be converted through the work. We should be encouraged to pray that God would show church members people with prepared hearts whom they can point to the Lord.

7. We need to teach our church people how they can use the Bible to lead someone to Christ.

8. We need breaks and holidays, but could we encourage not only young people but others as well to invest some of their holiday time in being involved with evangelistic work? Camps and beach missions, holiday clubs and other churches need helpers of all ages.

9. Church leadership should give careful thought to creatively using those with extra time or energy: some are unemployed; students may have long vacations; some are retired; some have seen their youngest start school and may be tempted to 'go back to work'; but each may be able to fit into a personalised outreach programme, helped and encouraged by the church, which will prove of great assistance in growth and service for the Lord.

10. There should be an active involvement in missionary work: missionary speakers, a wide range of missionary magazines and reports given in services and meetings. I was involved in a very small Evangelical

Church near Leeds where this policy was followed. Over ten years, thirteen people went into full-time Christian service in the UK or overseas.

'Go into all the world and preach the gospel to every creature,' said Jesus (Mk. 16:15). While a world perishes, millions do not know the way of salvation; but God has given us life, strength, energy and the knowledge of Himself. The great commission still stands. While we have breath to breathe and the means to make Christ known, let us give all we have and are to the joyful but demanding task of proclaiming Christ to those around us. Let us pray and work to see more little babes in the family. And may He have all the glory.

# Picture this – snapshots of effective evangelism

As Christians, we know the truth, and the truth will make us . . . odd! I'm not sure where I read that, but it could explain why evangelism is the Cinderella of evangelical experience.

We've heard the challenging messages and read the repeated pleas, but usually find ourselves on a guilt trip for not evangelising rather than experiencing the joy of sharing Jesus with others.

Could it be that we hear the voice of our neighbours more than the voice of God? They tell us to be silent, but He tells us to speak. Feeling intimidated, we can easily isolate ourselves from the non-Christians and spend all our free time with other Christians.

God still has a heart to save men and women. Throughout the Bible, God has shown that He wills that none 'should perish but that all should come to repentance' (2 Pet. 3:9). The greatest demonstration of this is the death and resurrection of the Lord Jesus Christ.

We are instructed by our Lord to 'Go . . . preach . . . and teach . . .' Surely the love of Christ constrains us to make known the good news of Christ. It was said of the socialist William Morris that he never saw a drunk without a feeling of personal responsibility for him, such was his compassion for humanity. How much more should we be moved with compassion at the needs of the crowds who are 'like sheep without a shepherd'?

What then can the church do? How can we use the weapons that God has given us to meet the needs of those around us? In the book of Acts there are three snapshots of evangelism which speak to our situation.

## The witness

First, there is the picture of the witness. The word is used as a verb or a noun twenty-nine times in Acts. 'But you shall receive power when the Holy Spirit has come upon you; and you shall be witnesses to Me in Jerusalem, and in all Judea and Samaria, and to the end of the earth' (Acts 1:8). There were to be ever-extending concentric circles of witness: first in Jerusalem, then Judea, then Samaria, the heathen world and eventually the uttermost parts of the earth. The early church took Christ's commission seriously, for we read, 'And daily in the temple, and in every house, they did not cease teaching and preaching Jesus as the Christ' (Acts 5:42). Six times in the book of Acts there is a progress report as to the effectiveness of their evangelism (6:7; 9:31; 12:24; 16:5; 19:20; 28:31). The gospel had reached the city of Rome within thirty years of Christ's resurrection.

Those early Christians were like the Methodists to whom it was said, 'You have nothing to do but to save souls, therefore spend and be spent in this work.'

Today, every Christian should be encouraged to witness to something he or she knows. Our words and actions should become almost irresistible. 'Witness' and 'martyr' are the same word in the Greek, indicating the committed Christian's willingness to die for being a faithful witness.

Do our churches consist of witnessing people? Could we actually lead a soul to Christ, as did Philip with the Ethiopian? When did we last have that joy? How many in our churches are actually witnessing? Do we have reports of personal work when we meet to pray? Are we encouraging people to speak about Jesus Christ? How real is our Christianity? Are we creatively thinking of ways into conversation with our friends and family? Are we praying for boldness and the Holy Spirit's help when these opportunities arise?

**The pastor**

Secondly, there is the picture of the pastor doing the work of the evangelist. It is hard to distinguish the prime gift of the apostle Paul. Though a church planter and pastor he was always working as an evangelist. He said, 'Woe is me if I preach not the gospel.' Paul's life is best summarised by the word 'witnessing'.

He refused to isolate himself in an ivory tower. Though a New Testament writer he would not give his life simply to study and writing. He was intimately involved in the lives and struggles of others. He wrote of ninety-nine different individuals in his letters (which in proportion to the numbers in the church at that time is quite incredible); he prayed continually for them, he brought before the Lord churches he knew and those he had never been with. He imitated his Saviour who preached to the masses and looked out for individuals.

Paul wrote to Timothy the pastor, 'Do the work of the evangelist.' The pastor has many responsibilities: he is to feed the flock of God, to pray, to lead, to comfort; but he must also act as an evangelist. The pastor is to strive to lead souls to Christ, not only through the public ministry, but in one-to-one encounters. Faithful pastors will not content themselves in only building up a congregation and expounding the Scriptures to them, invaluable as this is. The pastor will also be burdened to see people being led to Christ in repentance and faith.

I recently preached near Haddington and remembered John Brown, the orphan boy who had no schooling whatsoever and travelled five years as a pedlar; but after he was converted preached for thirty-six years. One sceptic said of him, 'He preached as though the Son of God stood at his elbow.' No wonder so many people were converted through his work.

A day later, I walked past St Peter's Church, Dundee, where Robert Murray McCheyne preached. Each Saturday he visited the dying to prepare his heart, so that on Sunday he might plead with souls the more earnestly. He said:

> I have not been like a shepherd after lost sheep, nor like a physician among dying men, nor like a servant bidding you to the marriage, nor like one plucking brands from the burning! How often have I gone to your houses to try and win souls, and you have put me off with a little worldly talk! I dared not tell you that you were perishing. How often have I sat at some of your tables, and my heart yearned for your souls, yet a false shame kept me silent! How often have I gone home crying bitterly, 'Free me from blood-guiltiness, O God!'

Pastors with an evangelistic burden are very effective tools in the hands of the Holy Spirit. Before preaching his unforgettable sermon 'Sinners in the hands of an angry God', Jonathan Edwards did not eat or sleep for three days. He repeatedly prayed, 'O Lord, give me New England.' Mrs Lloyd-Jones said, 'You will not understand my husband unless you see him first as an evangelist.'

One pastor friend of mine, a fine and careful Bible student and teacher, can be found outside the local supermarket twice each week, giving out tracts and seeking to talk to shoppers about the Lord. He's doing the work of an evangelist. Another friend who pastors a church is deeply involved with many on his estate, conducting one-to-one Bible studies with several non-Christians each week, and has done for years.

## The evangelist

The New Testament says, 'And He Himself gave some to be apostles, some prophets, some evangelists and some pastors and teachers, for the equipping of the saints for the work of the ministry, for the edifying of the body of Christ' (Eph. 4:11,12). There is no hint at all that the gift or calling of the evangelist has ceased.

Philip is specifically named as an evangelist and we see him witnessing to crowds and to individuals. He travelled, and then later stayed locally based (in Caesarea for twenty years). He preached the Word, focused attention on Christ and saw conversions to Christ.

Churches appoint pastors, assistants, youth pastors, music directors and so on. These people are sorely needed in our churches today. In fact, we need more pastors. It is such a blessing to have praying, studious, caring and evangelistic pastors. We also need evangelists: those with one primary sphere of ministry and duty.

Bible colleges train Bible teachers and pastors, and we desperately need them. The need for informed, educated and diligent pastors shouts at us from every local church.

But there is another call and it is from the world. We need evangelists. The fact is that it is rare for churches to appoint someone to the office and work of the evangelist, and it is rare for the Bible colleges to train them. I long to see our churches looking for, encouraging, training and using evangelists on a long-term basis for service in their own locality, and beyond.

Let us not forget that the supreme evangelist, the Lord Jesus said, 'Follow Me, and I will make you fishers of men' (Mt. 4:19).

# The crucified preacher

Every time I stand in front of a group of people to speak about Christ, I get stirred in my heart. What a privilege to share the gospel with men and women. There is no joy quite like it! Usually, I find myself engaged in conversation with people who want to know more, or have questions they are yearning to ask. However, sometimes the reaction of those who are listening is far from warm. I want to engage with all types of people, but to do so can be costly.

There are occasions when I have been frozen by the audience to whom I am speaking. In some school assemblies, or university bars, or even more traditional settings, there is an atmosphere you can feel, though nobody has said anything, that conveys the notion, 'We don't want to hear what you are saying.' Little or nothing is said afterwards, but you know that the gospel message has not gone down well. That inevitably creates an ache in the heart. Who doesn't want affirmation? A friend once said to me, 'Happiness is not in your job description!' And yet, everyone who is involved in proclaiming Christ, one-to-one, or one-to-a-crowd wants to believe that what has been said has been appreciated.

Moses knew the hurt of not being appreciated. 'He supposed that his brethren would understand that God was giving them salvation by his hand, but they did not understand' (Acts 7:25, see also vv. 39,51–53 and Ps.106:7, ESV). That misunderstanding cost him dearly.

The desire for affirmation can become so compelling that it is tempting to succumb to its lure. It starts with a process where one changes first some of the words and phrases, then the emphasis of the message and finally the message itself. It can happen very subtly. But it is dangerous, for we can find ourselves simply tickling itching ears.

There is another temptation to omit some less palatable aspects of the gospel, so that what one says is correct, but some key truths are simply never mentioned. It is all too easy to become, as C.S. Lewis said, a preacher who is *accommodating*, and water down the Word of God. Michael Watts in his booklet *Why the English Stopped Going to Church* argues that the decline in church attendance began around 1850, when the desire to be respected and reputable led to people avoiding teaching both hell and the substitutionary atonement of Christ.

## We die to what we preach

When Stephen preached in Acts 7, the crowd listened, until he faithfully applied the message. Then they turned against him, and he became the first Christian martyr. In Greek, the word 'witness' is based on the same word as 'martyr'. To preach faithfully means that we must be willing to die to self. Every preacher must deny himself, take up the cross and proclaim the Word of God. I have heard preachers who are great communicators, and even very funny comedians, who, to my mind at least, have not been faithful preachers of the Word. The words we proclaim must be spirit and life. It is not 'woe is me if I do not wow or woo the audience'.

It is not even 'woe is me if I do not preach what Jesus has done for me', but 'woe is me if I do not preach the gospel' (1 Cor. 9:16). Without fear or favour let us preach what God has given us, recognising that God is in the audience, and it is He whom we must please.

The greatest lesson in homiletics, the study of preaching, is that the preacher has to be willing to die to the clamour for the applause of the audience; the building of a good reputation; the excitement of giving 'a good word', and the thrill of knowing that one is regarded as a gifted preacher. 'For what we proclaim is not ourselves, but Jesus Christ as Lord, with ourselves as your servants for Jesus' sake' (2 Cor. 4:5, ESV). Oswald Chambers said: 'Never water down the word of God, preach it in its undiluted sternness; there must be unflinching loyalty to the word of God; but when you come to personal dealing with your fellow men, remember who you are – not a special being made up in heaven, but a sinner saved by grace.'

**We die to how we preach**

I would have loved to hear Paul preach, and if I had, I would have listened to a man who deliberately did not rely on himself, but on God who raises the dead (2 Cor. 1:9). He did not proclaim the testimony of God with lofty speech or wisdom. Instead he determined to know nothing among the people except Jesus Christ and Him crucified. He preached with weakness, and in fear, and with much trembling. His words were not in plausible words of wisdom, but in demonstration of the Spirit and . . . power (1 Cor. 2:1–4). His authority and power rested not in his method of preaching, but in the source of his message, which was the Word of God.

This does not mean that we should not prepare to communicate well. It does mean that our dependence is upon God, and not on ourselves. God knows what is the truth, and we are presumptuous if we feel we can juggle the words and themes of the Bible to make them more palatable to today's audience. The preacher must never be a detractor from Jesus, but one who cries in clear, certain and compassionate words, 'Behold! The Lamb of God who takes away the sin of the world' (Jn. 1:29.)

Neither does it mean that because I have the truth of God's Word, I can speak aggressively and arrogantly. We read of the Lord that He did not shout or cry out in the street (Is. 42:2). He was tender, compassionate and winsome, and so we should be. Humility should adorn the Christian preacher, whose authority comes from God and not from himself, his studies or his abilities. 'This is what God says' will be his watchword.

Humour, anecdotes, illustrations, alliteration, balanced sentences and a host of other means of attracting and keeping attention are surely right, but they must never be a means of drawing attention to the preacher rather than the Lord. And if appreciation is given at the end of a message, then we give the Lord all the glory. Corrie Ten Boom, the Dutch Christian who survived Ravensbruck, when thanked after she had spoken, received the appreciation as if she had been given a rose. At the end of a day she would love to present to the Lord a bouquet of roses, recognising that all she had been able to do was because of the Lord.

## We die to whom we preach

If the preacher is to die to self, it will affect where they minister, as well as how they minister. The Lord preached in cities and to large crowds, but also in villages and to individuals. It is wonderful to be given large opportunities. However, it is my conviction that as so much Christian activity (at least in the UK) is done in small works, it is right to go to the struggling causes as well as the successful ones; to go to small Christian Unions, as well as those bursting at the seams.

Also, dying to self means that the preacher will proclaim the gospel to the poor as well as the wealthy. Everyone has the right to hear the good news of Jesus. We are neither to neglect the affluent, nor turn away from the cry of the poor. Heaven will be filled with people from every tribe and language and people and nation, and every class and intellectual ability. The church is not an exclusive group, nor is it a club. The Lord is able to supply all our needs, and He can make up the 'losses' for the times when what we receive does not cover costs incurred.

Our aim in proclaiming is not to impress, but to simply express eternal truth so that all may hear and understand. Martin Luther said, 'When I preach I regard neither doctors nor magistrates, of whom I have above forty in my congregation; I have all my eyes on the servant maids and on their children. And if the learned men are not well-pleased with what they hear, well, the door is open.'

### We die to when we preach

Paul's final charge to young Timothy was to 'Preach the word! Be ready in season and out of season' (2 Tim. 4:2). I have known preachers who proclaim their word, and then walk by those who listened, unwilling to talk to any of them. Proclamation, though, is as much one-to-one, when there is a seeking or hurting soul, as it is speaking to the crowds. To break the hard heart or heal the broken one is exhausting work, but it is what we are called to do. And what better way to spend and be spent? It may be that we will come to an age in life when we are too old to be preaching in pulpits, but there never comes a time when we are to be silent about the Lord. Again, Paul, a pattern believer, at the end of his life in Rome, from morning until evening expounded, testified and persuaded people about the Lord from the Word.

Isaiah preached faithfully and was sawn in half. Jeremiah preached faithfully and was mocked and imprisoned. John the Baptist preached faithfully and was beheaded. Stephen preached faithfully and was stoned to death. Ridley and Latimer and a host of others in Europe preached faithfully and were burned at the stake. Richard Wurmbrandt preached faithfully and was put in solitary confinement for fourteen years. If we proclaim faithfully, we too will have to die, at least to self, and perhaps to more. The Lord, who made Himself of no reputation and went to the cross, tells of the blessing there is in dying to self: 'Unless a grain of wheat falls into the earth and dies, it remains alone, but if it dies, it bears much fruit. Whoever loves his life loses it, and whoever hates his life in this world will keep it for eternal life' (Jn. 12:24,25, ESV).

# Evangelism – the individual believer's part

Most Christians I know deplore the idea of monastic life. We rightly believe that as Christians we are to be salt and light, and that involves contact with unconverted people. And yet, time and again while preparing churches for mission, I am told by Christians that they do not have non-Christian friends. In practice, it appears that we have misread the Scriptures, which tell us to be separate from the world, as 'Come out from among them and become isolated . . .' The instruction in 2 Corinthians 6:17 tells us to be different, not to be detached.

So what is happening to us that we are missing out on the huge joy of meeting with, befriending, praying for, witnessing to and winning men and women to Jesus Christ? Perhaps we feel intimidated by their antagonism to the gospel, or frustrated and disappointed by their indifference, or perhaps just frightened lest we let down the Lord by our life, or weak example. Could it be that we have become so wrapped up in our group of Christian friends or church activities we are neglecting reaching out to unconverted people?

**Life is so daily!**

The American evangelist, D.L. Moody, never let a day go by without speaking to some unsaved person about Jesus Christ. My New Year resolution this year was to open my pocket Bible as frequently as possible and share it with non-Christian people I meet. I know Christians who have the wonderful ability of turning ordinary conversations into significant ones for the Lord; they go from small talk to big talk. I am convinced that this is not just a gift for the particularly gifted few. Rather it is a challenge that all we who love the Lord can take to ourselves.

If we believe that each individual was made in the image of God and has an endless existence in heaven or hell, then it will be evident that the good news of the gospel is the most important and urgent message for every individual to hear. 'The grace of God has appeared to all men, bringing salvation for all people', but to be saved, they have to hear that message. And the most effective preachers are we ordinary Christians going about our daily lives. Therefore, as we begin each new day, let us ask God to help us speak to someone about the gospel, and then look for opportunities.

**The people we meet**

Most of us are constantly meeting different people: the shop assistant, the waiter, the postman, the person who stands next to us in a queue, or sits next to us on a bus or train, the colleague or family member, and even the telephone salesperson! Some of these we will never meet again, others are regular contacts who we can befriend and care for. Each of them needs to hear the good news that 'Christ Jesus came into the world to save sinners' (1 Tim. 1:15). So, let us be alert for opportunities to chatter about the Lord. I have found that a tract can be the key to open the door of conversation with those I will not meet again. For neighbours and friends, I prayerfully wait for the 'right' moment to speak. Personal work like this is much easier when it is done one-to-one, and when the person to whom we are speaking begins to ask questions. We then have the privilege of praying for the people to whom we have spoken. Eric Alexander said, 'The primary evangelistic method is prayer.' It may be that you will be the only person who will ever pray for that particular individual.

The sin of the rich man of whom Jesus spoke in Luke 16, was that he neglected his neighbour. Our 'neighbours' are those we meet, and they are a wonderful mission field, provided we are genuine, prayerful and winsome in our approach to them. If church activities dominate our lives, then we have to go out of our way to make friends with non-Christians. I took a church mission where unusually large numbers of unconverted people attended. The church administrator explained why, saying that though it is not a condition of membership, there was an emphasis on each member of the church to join something secular in town. (It could be a PTA, or watercolour painting class, reading group, sports club, foreign language course – there are endless options!) 'Therefore, everyone has non-Christian friends, so that they can all bring people along to events such as a mission.'

## Paul's requests for prayer

The apostle Paul was not ashamed to ask others to pray for him. And when he did, he expressed his longing both for a door of opportunity to open for him to proclaim the gospel, and for boldness to speak. Have you noticed how life is so daily? Following Paul's example, let us, at the start of every day, ask God to lead us to people who need to hear the good news of Jesus and His love. Then, as we proceed, it is all about having an evangelistic mindset. We will find that speaking to people about the Lord grows to become a joyful passion, and that the Lord is using us to point men and women to Christ.

### Individuals in church

A church functioning as it should will have a strategy and programme of prayer and evangelism. There should be carefully thought through plans to reach every type of person in each corner of the locality. This will mean that individual Christians will be able to use their gifts in reaching the community in a variety of ways. The church will want to encourage its members to use what gifts God has given them to evangelise the community.

### Creative evangelism

There are so many different creative ways we can use our talents and personalities to reach out to others. A pot of tea or freshly brewed coffee can be used as an evangelistic means to build the bridge and befriend people. I have known people use their homes as a venue for suppers with a guest speaker explaining the gospel. One sixth-former when leaving school had sixty-five students and teachers for a barbecue in his back garden with a gospel talk to conclude the event. Another put on a music evening with young people playing various instruments, and testifying of their trust in Christ to a packed church. Others have led their friends through a *Christianity Explored* course to great effect.

It is a joy to see Christians setting up Christian Unions in schools, FE colleges, universities and workplaces, reaching out to others, testifying to all of their Christian commitment, and encouraging other believers in their walk with God. I have been to some fine Christmas carol services held in workplaces, where many unsaved colleagues of Christians have heard the gospel.

## Influential people?

Six years after Jesus gave the commission to go into all the world and preach the gospel, Stephen was to become the first Christian martyr. This led to the early Christians being scattered, while the church leaders stayed in the difficult situation in Jerusalem. These anonymous believers were used to spread the Christian message. Their names do not appear in our Bible, but what they did was vital, impacted the world for good, and was noted in heaven. Ours is the same commission, and if we are used to win souls, we will not only be wise, but involved in the great ongoing tide of the spread of the gospel. In one hundred years time, our names may not appear in *Time* magazine's most influential people list, but we will have been involved in the most significant work there is to do here on earth, that of reaching people for Jesus.

# Great communicator; no gospel

A friend recently attended a major evangelistic event for students. There were over eight hundred people present. When I asked him how it went, he replied that it proved to be a great opportunity, but then added of the speaker, 'A great communicator, but no gospel. He simply did not preach the cross.' Warren Wiersbe in an article entitled 'No News is Bad News' said: 'We have heard well-outlined sermons, based on careful exegesis, that did not proclaim the gospel or even mention the name of Jesus! And they were preached not in liberal churches but in evangelical churches.'

We have to remember that it is only the body of Christ who will faithfully proclaim the good news of the gospel. There is no other group or organisation committed to doing that. Whatever size of congregation, those listening are likely to be educated, shrewd people, whose expectations of us will be great. However, that is no reason for proclaiming anything other than Christ and Him crucified. Christ alone, not wise and eloquent words, or even erudite exposition, can save, feed and bless the soul. As someone has observed, 'The good news did not fit Jesus' times or His world.' G.K. Chesterton had it right when he said, 'If the Church marries the spirit of the age, she will soon become a widow.' We are to proclaim Christ and Him crucified.

**A definite Christ**

I would have loved to have heard the Apostle Paul preach. He can at least mentor us, through his letters. To the Corinthians he wrote: 'For I determined not to know anything among you except Jesus Christ and Him crucified' (1 Cor. 2:2). He deliberately sought to exclude from his preaching and the enthusiasms of his mind everything but that great central truth. The crucifixion and resurrection are the heart of the gospel. If we have the choice of great eloquence, or true faithfulness, then our pride ought to be laid on the Lord's altar, as we depend on his truth to do its eternal work.

There is a real Christ, who was born, lived, died and rose again. And as a Puritan expressed it, 'He who rose from the clods, we expect from the clouds.' Jesus was as much a man as a man can be; and as much God as God can be. Christ is the beginning, middle and end of our salvation. All the blessings of God come to us through Christ. As Christians, we love Him. So let us proclaim Him. I have found that when I focus on Christ, quiet stillness often descends on the listeners. I believe that the Holy Spirit delights to honour the Lord Jesus. And, even in this secular age, I am sure that there is still something very appealing about Christ.

The twentieth-century American preacher, Vance Havner, told the story of two boats which were passing each other on the Mississippi River when an old black man said to a white passenger as he pointed to the other boat, 'Look, yonder's the captain!' When asked for an explanation, he said, 'Years ago, we were goin' along like this and I fell overboard and the captain rescued me. And since then, I just loves to point him out!' Surely we feel this way about Christ. Since trusting in Him, He has won our hearts, and we want to speak of Him. Let us do so with fresh vigour. He has been lifted up on the cross, so He will draw people to Himself.


## A definite cross

The cross of Jesus did not just happen to Christ, He came for the very purpose of dying as our atoning sacrifice. The cross is indispensable. Our Creator took on Himself flesh and suffered and died. God 'laid on Him the iniquity of us all' (Is. 53:6). He 'bore our sins in His own body on the tree' (1 Pet. 2:24); 'And He Himself is the propitiation for our sins, and not for ours only but also for the whole world' (1 Jn. 2:2). He died, 'the Just for the unjust, that He might bring us to God' (1 Pet. 3:18). The Bible makes so much of the Christ crucified, because it reveals the very heart of God. The hymn expresses this well

> It is a thing most wonderful,
> Almost too wonderful to be
> That God's own Son should come from
>     heaven
> And die to save a child like me.
>
> *William Walsham How (1823–1897)*

Jesus is the Lamb slain before the foundation of the world – so the gospel of Christ has been in God's heart throughout eternity. Christ's sacrifice for our sins is our only means of salvation. All the blessings of God come through Jesus and Him crucified. Four times the New Testament tells the story of the death of Christ, and though sparing the detail, these narratives are weighty in their theology. Therefore any preaching or doctrine which is not embedded in the cross is bound to lead us astray.

In reality, to fail to proclaim the cross is to be a traitor to the gospel.

## A definite conclusion

If Christ and Him crucified is true, then the only conclusion is that we, like Paul, will be determined to know nothing else. My responsibility is not to tickle the ears of listeners by fancy thoughts, stories or jokes. Let others be political if they wish. Let others rummage for new ideas or controversies, which may even hit the headlines of the Christian press. Let others charm their hearers and become 'pleasers of men'. C.S. Lewis said that he didn't go to religion to make him happy; he always knew a bottle of port would do that! He said that if someone wanted a religion to make them feel really comfortable, he would not recommend Christianity.

Message by message I want to pave the way to the cross and use words and every fibre of my being to point people to the One who suffered and died on Calvary's cross and is now risen and alive. We need to explain to all the hidden work of Christ, that He bore our sins in His own body on the tree – He died as the sin-bearer, and substitute for sin. I plead that in all our evangelistic preaching we present Christ, and the significance of His great work on the cross. Speaking of His death on the cross, Jesus said, 'But I, when I am lifted up from the earth, will draw all men to myself' (Jn. 12:32, NIV).

Once an individual hears of the loving appeal of Jesus dying on the cross, he or she begins to find there is something there which answers the cry of individual hearts, as well as the deepest needs of the world. What we have to do as God's servants is to make much of Christ and Him crucified. Charles Haddon Spurgeon was only twenty-one years old when he said, 'Calvary preaching: Calvary theology, Calvary books, Calvary sermons! These are the things we want. And in proportion as we have Calvary exalted and Christ magnified, the gospel is preached.' Of course, there are different styles of preachers, and varying personalities will present truth in a variety of ways; but as David Larsen expressed it, 'No two violinists will play a symphony exactly the same, but the brilliance and genius of the composer will be set forth by the faithful artist. This is the task of the gospel proclaimer: to process and package the truth of the evangel for listeners of our time.'[18]

Praise the Lord for great communicators, but my prayer is for more gospel preachers. Let us be determined to know nothing but Jesus: Christ and Him crucified.

# Great expectations

I heard a sermon recently on the theme 'One hundred years of evangelism from a personal point of view'. The well-respected preacher began by outlining the story of his grandfather, converted in the dockyards of Glasgow, who became an effective soul-winner. He was Arminian in theology as an evangelist and later a pastor, and saw people converted right to the end of his life. He was loved by all, and could recall great stories of God's working through him for the salvation of others.

Developing his theme, the preacher described his father who pastored a number of churches, was greatly loved, and was a passionate preacher of the Word. In the early days, we were told, he saw much fruit, but gradually this diminished, so that at the end of years of ministry he was bewailing the fact that there was comparatively little fruit. We were told that over the years he had gradually moved from an Arminian to a Calvinist position, much through the influence of Dr Martyn Lloyd-Jones.

Finally, the preacher told us about himself. Currently, he pastors what he described as a 'successful' church, which by English standards, is above average size. He is a Calvinist, and while recognising that his gifting is that of a pastor-teacher, feels concerned that very, very few 'outsiders' are converted through either his ministry, or the work of the church which he pastors.

This is not the place to discuss the doctrines of free will and predestination. I am well aware that God has greatly used Calvinists such as Whitefield, McCheyne and Spurgeon, as well as Arminians like Wesley, Finney and Booth. Personally, I feel deeply wary of human systems imposed on the Scripture. Emerson said, 'Beware of a systems-maker.'

But why has there been this decline in fruitfulness? Why has our nation so unapologetically rejected the Christ whom we dearly love? Our answers are well rehearsed. One could argue that in Western Europe today the Christian message is hardly in vogue. Evangelicals are often held in derision by the media, disbelieved by the majority who want to live their own lives undisturbed by warnings of judgement, despised by academics and marginalised by leaders of society and media manipulators. Assailed by false teachers who water down or pollute the message of the gospel, we feel we are up against it – it will never be an easy task to evangelise our nation. We even wonder whether it is God's doing, thinking that He has withdrawn His hand of blessing from the nation. We know from Scripture that He has done this in the past, but I fear this particular argument, lest we blame God for our own lack of faith.

However, let us not forget that the gospel has not changed. According to Romans 1:16 ('I am not ashamed of the gospel, because it is the power of God for the salvation of everyone who believes . . .' NIV), the gospel is not merely an idea to be shared or a philosophy to be discussed, but a power to be unleashed. Furthermore, the Lord's arm has not become shortened so that it cannot save, nor his heart hardened that he does not want to! We read, 'The Lord is not slack concerning His promise . . . not willing that any should perish, but that all should come to repentance' (2 Pet. 3:9). And again, '"As

I live," says the Lord GOD, "I have no pleasure in the death of the wicked, but that the wicked turn from his way and live"' (Ezek. 33:11). 'God our Saviour . . . desires all people to be saved and to come to the knowledge of the truth' (1 Tim. 2:3,4). Jesus said, 'How often I wanted to gather [you] . . . but you were not willing' (Mt. 23:37).

And let us be reminded that men and women who are unsaved are usually aware that they are guilty of wrongdoing, even if their standard of right and wrong is not God's. They often fear death. Conscience is the evangelists' ally, so that as God's holiness is proclaimed, there is an inward voice in the hearer confirming the truth of their own guilt. Then the Holy Spirit Himself convicts people of sin, judgement and righteousness to come. God still answers prayer, and lovingly appeals to all to 'Come to Me, all you who labour and are heavy laden, and I will give you rest' (Mt. 11:28).

When I meet an unsaved person, I am totally convinced that he or she should and could be converted. Whatever their background, degree of interest, or understanding about the things of God, I believe they can be saved. I am not claiming to have great faith, or unusual discernment, but believing Christ died for them, I love to 'offer to them Christ' (as John Wesley so often described his preaching). The gospel invitation is open to all, and I cannot believe that God would merely be going through the exercise of inviting all, if all could not respond.

Proclaiming the gospel, we tell people that the God who made them is holy, just, trustworthy and loving. We explain their need to repent; that God commands all men and women everywhere to repent – to turn from their sins and trust Christ. It is our duty to make much of the fact that God came into the world, and went to the cross to bear in His own body the sin of the world, and how the risen Jesus can become their Lord, Saviour and Friend. We should urge them to consider this earnestly, because their eternal destiny depends on whether they repent and believe in Jesus.

The words on the plinth of John Bunyan's statue in Bedford are, 'He pleaded with men'. Having presented the gospel, we ask the listener(s) to respond by turning from their sin in repentance and trusting Christ by faith. Let us explain what they must do, as we call them to the Jesus who invited all to come to Him.

Because we have prayed that the Lord would bring us into contact with people whose hearts have been pre-pared by Him, we can expect some of these people to be converted. Such confidence would be naïve except that the Lord has said, 'Those who sow in tears shall reap in joy. He who continually goes forth weeping, Bearing seed for sowing, shall doubtless come again with rejoic-ing, Bringing his sheaves with him' (Ps. 126:5,6). We long to see many more trusting the Saviour, and we bewail the apathy and antagonism which often charac-terise those with whom we share the things of Christ. Nevertheless, there are the most joyful moments when we are privileged to lead people to the Saviour. Let us pray for revival, but whether or not we have one, we continue to work hard presenting Christ to all.

Is expectation a missing dimension in our evangelism? Have doctrinal systems inadvertently straitjacketed us so that we have been robbed of a sense of expectation? Or, conversely, has a lack of expectation led us to doctrinal systems which excuse our lack of fruitfulness? After all, the farmer sows in anticipation that he will in due time reap, and the businessman invests with hope that in time he will profit. So should we not proclaim Christ, with the assurance that the Holy Spirit will use our words to save men and women? The story is told of a young pastor moaning to Spurgeon, 'I'm troubled. Sunday by Sunday I preach but nobody is converted.' Spurgeon replied, 'Well, you don't expect people to be converted every week, do you?' 'No,' replied the young man. 'And that is why they are not,' was the quick response from the sage! Lack of expectation is a form of a lack of faith.

When Elisha had fallen sick with the illness from which he was to die, Joash, king of Israel, went down to him and wept. Elisha told him to take a bow and arrow and shoot eastwards. Then he commanded him to take the arrows and strike the land with them, which he did, but only three times. Elisha was angry. 'You should have struck five or six times; then you would have struck Syria till you had destroyed! But now you will strike down Syria only three times' (2 Kgs. 13:19). The faith and persistence of Joash had fallen short, and he was to be deprived of the victories he had sought.

Whatever name we tag on to our lack of faith, I believe we should repent of it. It destroys the vibrancy that should be evident in the life of the church and individual Christians. Let us claim and live by the promises of God, and go out into the world attempting and expecting great things from God. For we are told that 'Whoever abides in me and I in him, he it is that bears much fruit' (Jn. 15:5, ESV).

Let us remember the words of Jesus to the two blind men (Mt. 9:29, ESV), 'According to your faith be it done to you.'

# The priority of evangelism – Acts 28:16–31

The apostle Paul is a pattern Christian. He is not our Lord or Saviour, but he is a great example of what it means to be a believer. As far as evangelism is concerned, his example of strategic, fervent, faithful proclamation of Christ is second to none. Even at the end of his life, by example he is setting out essential principles of the priority of evangelism.

Paul had always wanted to go to Rome to personally preach the gospel there. Instead he arrived as a prisoner. It was not so much that Paul said, 'I must go . . . to Rome' (Acts 19:21, NLT), but rather that Jesus had said, 'you must . . . testify in Rome' (Acts 23:11, NIV), though Paul didn't know that he would be a prisoner there. All circumstances were calculated to make Paul's trip to Rome impossible: the forces of nature, the wiles of men and Satan were against Paul, but eventually he had safe conduct to the capital of the Roman Empire. It was probably his last journey. Paul repeatedly described himself as 'the prisoner of the Lord' (not the prisoner of Caesar, or the Roman guard, but of the Lord). And in prison we see that Paul was:

## 1. Evangelistic to the end

Evangelism is proclaiming the gospel to non-Christians who are listening. At the end of Acts we find Paul in prison under house arrest. There would have been restrictions but, at least to begin with, Paul was given great freedoms, which he turned into opportunities to make Christ known. It would have been easy for Paul to feel that the situation was too difficult, and that he had already 'done his stint'. Rather, with a deep-seated recognition that men and women were lost, without hope and destined to hell, Paul had to speak. In Colossians 4:3 Paul asked for prayer that: 'God would open to us a door for the word, to speak the mystery of Christ.' The prison door may have been closed, but it was an open door of opportunity, which interested Paul.

In Acts 28:23 we read three verbs, which give us a clue as to what evangelism is all about. Paul explained, testified or declared and tried to convince or persuade. In verse 31 we read that he preached the kingdom of God and about the Lord Jesus Christ. The backcloth of the whole of the Bible, and the foundation of all Christian belief is 'Christ and Him crucified', and so our aim should be to pave the way to explaining who Jesus is and how He carried and paid for our sins in His death and resurrection. Then we can testify as to what God has personally done for us and in us, and then persuade people to respond to the claims of Christ on their lives.

Ours are difficult days, with increased apathy and antagonism to the true and living God. But Rome at the time of Paul was not exactly eager to hear of their need to repent and believe. Similarly, Titus was not given an easy task when he went to Crete to reach the people and establish elders, in a place where the people were 'liars, evil beasts, lazy gluttons' (Tit. 1:12).

When John Wesley arrived in Newcastle he was appalled by the wickedness of the city. He wrote in his Journal on 28 May 1742

> We came to Newcastle about six; and after short refreshment, walked into the town. I was surprised: so much drunkenness, cursing and swearing (even from the mouths of little children), do I never remember to have seen and heard before in so small a compass of time. Surely this place is ripe for Him who came not to call the righteous, but sinners to repentance!

God knew what He was doing with Paul, for in prison he actually found that his witness was expanded, enriched and authenticated by his suffering. Tough as it was, Paul's evangelism was used and people were converted.

## 2. Creative in his means

Paul became 'an ambassador in chains'. He devised means to create evangelistic openings. First, he appealed to the people who would at least listen to what he had to say. He called together local Jewish leaders. We know too that he witnessed to the prison guard, and that the message spread throughout the palace household (Phil. 4:22). He probably stood before the world's most prestigious person, in the world's most prestigious court, and faithfully proclaimed Christ.

Whenever the early Christians appeared before the authorities, they saw it as an opportunity to witness! If it is true that the most important message is that of Christ crucified and risen, then the most urgent requirement for every Christian is to get that message out, by all legitimate means, to every person. Every aspect of our lives is to have an evangelistic dimension, whether at work, home, church, free time or holidays.

There will of course, be a different approach to the various people with whom we have contact, but the greatest act of friendship and kindness we can show to anyone is to tell them about Christ, and introduce them to Him. We may have to fight the temptation to cut ourselves off from contact and friendship with unconverted people.

## 3. Biblical in his message

There is no special gospel for modern people. The same message, which is the theme of the Bible, is just as relevant today as ever. The authority for the message is derived from the Word of God. As we proclaim the gospel, we are not simply sharing an idea or philosophy but unleashing a power, for the gospel is 'the power of God for salvation'.

God has promised to bless the proclamation of His Word (Is. 55:10,11). I carry a Bible with me always, and as often as possible I like to open it and show passages to the people with whom I am talking.

When the Word of God is proclaimed either one-to-one, or one to a crowd, God the Holy Spirit takes hold of it and brings life out of death – new birth! This is what happened when Ezekiel preached to the valley of dry bones, and it still happens today when Christians get out the gospel to non-Christians who are listening. Remember that the sower sows the Word. Peter wrote, 'If anyone speaks, he should do it as one speaking the very words of God' (1 Pet. 4:11, NIV), and Paul instructed Timothy to 'Preach the Word', not just homilies and jokes! There may be different ways of preaching the Bible (in the past Luther, Calvin, Spurgeon, Billy Graham, Lloyd-Jones – all preached the Bible, though they did it very differently to each other), but it must be the Bible which is being proclaimed. The Reformation was largely due to a copy of the Scripture left in seclusion in a monastery. There it was hidden until Martin Luther came under its influence and its truths gripped him.

Our confidence is in the God of the Scripture to use His Word, though our responsibility is to connect with the unconverted and apply the message. We have nothing to apologise about, nothing to be ashamed of, but everything to be bold about.

### Fruitful in his preaching

The power in evangelism is the cross of our Lord Jesus Christ and the transforming effect of the gospel. Time and again, John Wesley would note in his journal at the end of a day, 'I gave them Christ.'

When we proclaim the Word in a way that connects with human minds and hearts, we are

- Sending out a light (2 Cor. 4:6; Ps. 119:130).
- Planting the seed (Lk. 8:4–8).
- Giving the medicine (Ps. 107:20).
- Wielding the sword (Heb. 4:12; Eph. 6:17).
- Serving the food (Mt. 4:4, 1 Pet. 2:2, Jer. 15:16).
- Applying the water (Jn. 15:3; Eph. 5:25–27).
- Holding up a mirror so that people can see Christ and be transformed into his image (2 Cor. 3:17,18).

We should expect God to do His work, and bring people to the point where they are willing to repent and believe the gospel. We sow, expecting that in due season we will reap. Needless to say, that as well as expecting the blessing of conversions, there will be opposition. It has always been like that. Jehoiakim burnt Jeremiah's scroll, cutting it up with a knife and casting it into a cauldron. But Jeremiah kept on proclaiming the Word.

Paul used the Scripture, even when speaking against those who were rejecting the Word and the gospel. In a prison cell, at the end of his life, Paul was involved in what had become his lifestyle, that whatever else he may have 'done for a living', he existed to proclaim Christ.

Living to make Christ known, and to win people to Jesus Christ, may not bring acclaim from the world. In a hundred years from now, we may be forgotten, but we will have been involved in the greatest work – that of bringing people to Jesus. And that lasts for eternity.

# John on his mentor John, in the Gospel of John

I had read the Gospel of John several times, but somehow missed the verses at the end of chapter 10 until I spotted them on a gravestone! I was in Bangor in Northern Ireland and went to see the grave of a friend murdered by the IRA and, very near to it, that of W.P. Nicholson, who was so greatly used by the Lord to win thousands to Christ over fifty years ago. Engraved on his gravestone were the words

> John did no miracle, but all that John said about (Jesus) was true. And many believed on Him there.

John the Gospel-writer had been a follower of John the Baptist, but had left to become a disciple of Jesus. John had always esteemed John the Baptist greatly, referring to him several times in his Gospel. The mention in chapter 10 is the final reference to him. John is given high praise, yet shown to be subordinate to Christ. (Successive references to John the Baptist from chapter 1 through to 10 in John's Gospel are shorter – a curious illustration of John the Baptist's own words regarding Jesus that 'He must increase; I must decrease').

Jesus had left Jerusalem, which He was not to visit again until Palm Sunday, three or four months later.

He went to Bethany, beyond Jordan, where John had borne testimony to Jesus at the beginning of Jesus' public ministry. It was here that the crowds came to Jesus and the words above were said. There are at least three insights I learn about John from these verses:

## 1. What he did was simple – 'John did no miracle'

There was nothing sensational about John's life and ministry. His lifestyle could not have been more humble, and his preaching was far from self-centred. No miracles were done, nor attempted, nor needed. His concern was not whether or not he was living a great life, but rather to point people to Jesus. It was preaching Christ that made him great in the sight of God. However, we who trust in Christ crucified and risen experience something more wonderful, such that even John did not enter in to (see Mt. 11:11).

It was Jesus who was to perform miracles, and the Gospel of John makes much of them. The signs of Jesus which John points out give authenticity to Jesus' claims of deity. They demonstrated the truth of who Jesus is. John the Baptist did not focus attention on himself, but on Jesus, so there were no miracles.

In a media-manipulated society let us not fall into the trap of believing that the sensational, which attracts attention, is what pleases the Lord. It may not be. To simply obey Jesus; to live lives uncluttered by the things that seem both attractive and even necessary; to spend time with Jesus and speak of Him, are of great price in the sight of the Lord.

## 2. What he said was true – 'all that he said about Jesus was true'

As a herald, it was John's duty to raise his voice in repeated proclamation of the King. John did little else than speak of Jesus, but this was sufficient. It was all that he was required to do.

> He spoke of Jesus privately – to two disciples as they stood beside Him. He also spoke publicly to crowds, which included soldiers and tax collectors. And all that he said was true.
>
> John said that Jesus was from heaven, and is above all: and that was true.
>
> John said that Jesus was the bridegroom of all men and women who trusted Him as their Lord and Saviour: and that was true.
>
> John said that the Father would not give the Spirit by measure to Jesus: and that was true.
>
> John said that His winnowing fan would be in His hand, and He would thoroughly purge His floor: and that was true.
>
> John said that He would be the Lamb of God who would take away the sin of the world: and that was true.

What John had said prophetically, we can declare knowing that in time and history, 'Christ died for our sins according to the Scriptures, and that He was buried, and that He rose again the third day according to the Scriptures' (1 Cor. 15:3,4).

It is our responsibility to ensure that what we are proclaiming is 'the truth, the whole truth and nothing but the truth', then God will help us as we tell others about Jesus. Trying to be politically correct and inoffensive in our witnessing robs us of God's blessing, and in effect says that we know better than God in what to communicate. God uses the people who have confidence in Him and His Word. We must communicate in twenty-first century language, relevantly, prayerfully, passionately and *truthfully*.

## 3. What he accomplished was significant – 'Many believed on Him there'

In his lifetime, John saw people repent, believe and be baptised. Yet there was more. The incident here at the end of John 10 happened at least two years after the martyrdom of John the Baptist. Clearly, his words and witness remained in the people's minds and hearts, for it was they who made this comment. This in itself is enough of a miracle in which to be glad. It is a very precious thing to be able to give thoughts and truths about Christ that cause people to consider Him, and to believe in Him.

God honoured John's faithfulness with fruitfulness. Despite the indifference towards the Lord that we daily encounter, we should expect to see fruit. Our age may not be easy, but neither was John's. He was beheaded for speaking the truth, and Jesus was crucified. Today we face both apathy and antagonism, but there are those who want to know the meaning of life, and the way to peace with God. Wouldn't it be wonderful if this year we could each be involved in meeting someone who is to believe in the Lord through our witness? Surely, it would be *the* highlight of the year!

# Attractive evangelism

I recently spoke at the opening of a church in Birmingham where the pastor was a converted Hindu. He, his brothers, a sister and his parents had been converted after the sudden death of his 22-year-old brother. He, also a Hindu, had been converted through a tract which had been given to him when he was about to go to a Jehovah's Witnesses Kingdom Hall. Outside, somebody was distributing Christian tracts, and this young man had taken one, read it, gone to a Baptist church and been converted.

In Mussleborough I interviewed a man in his forties converted through reading tracts that had been sent in pre-paid envelopes to the Royal Mail in Edinburgh where he was working. He had had no other contact with the gospel.

One of Britain's leading pastors was converted through reading the Gospel of Mark. It was tucked under his windscreen wiper in Austria. When he returned from a day of mountain climbing, he read it and became a follower of Christ.

A man, who for twenty-seven years had been working in Argentina, returned to his home in Sheffield for one month. He found a gospel booklet in a telephone kiosk, read it and trusted the Lord.

Ninety-four per cent of the population of England and Wales do not go to any type of church. A large proportion do not know any real Christian at all. So how shall they hear without a preacher? One way is through the gospel tract. How else can we reach people normally out of reach of the church? Who reaches the masses of young people who spend the weekend clubbing? How do we share Christ with those who have no Christian background? At least a tract may lead to a conversation. A few minutes before writing this article I gave a booklet to a Muslim shopkeeper; we engaged in a few minutes of conversation about the Lord,which was not very productive, but it may be more than he has ever had before.

'Give me twenty-six lead soldiers and I'll conquer the world', said Benjamin Franklin. Printing is much easier today, but distribution of what is printed still takes effort. Oswald Smith expressed how I feel: 'For more than thirty years I have prayerfully considered the problem, "How can we evangelise the world in a space of one generation?" . . . There must be a way. After travel and study in 53 countries I have come to this conclusion – the only way we are going to be able to carry out the Great Commission will be by means of the printed page.'

We have become all too familiar with publications that spread evil. John Angell James, one of England's revered Christians of the past, as an old man said that he had never fully recovered from the ill effects of fifteen minutes' reading of a bad leaflet when he was a boy. In contrast Hudson Taylor read a tract at the age of fifteen, and the five words, 'The finished work of Christ' were to change his life for ever, which in turn would make an impact on the whole of China. It was a pamphlet written by Martin Luther that fell into the hands of John Bunyan, and was the means of his conversion.

From his pen came *Pilgrim's Progress* through which thousands have been saved. Who knows the impact of a prayerfully distributed tract today? You remember how the verse 'Cast your bread upon the waters . . .' (Ecc. 11:1) ends? It says, 'For you will find it after many days.' Elsewhere in the Bible we read, 'Those who sow in tears Shall reap in joy. He who continually goes forth weeping, bearing seed for sowing, shall *doubtless* come again with rejoicing bringing his sheaves with him' (Ps. 126:5,6 my italics).

A tract or booklet, given away, is like an evangelist or missionary. It never shows cowardice or compromise. It does not get discouraged. It can equally reach the poor or the aristocracy. It can faithfully declare the Word of life; it does not answer back or become irritated when ignored. Prayerfully used, it can be read in quietness or in the bustle of a busy life, at all times of the day or night. It can be left untouched for years before being picked up, read and used by God. These 'evangelists' need our prayerful backing!

Tracts – or Christian leaflets, as I prefer to call them – need not be drab, weird, old-fashioned or have the appearance of a mass of print. They can be attractive, well-designed and endearing to the gospel. Prayerfully used, they need not be discarded. Could I make two suggestions?

## 1. Use tracts

Could I encourage you to always carry a tract or a gospel booklet with you?[19] It can be the door to open conversation about the things of God. For example, when buying petrol, if there isn't a queue behind you, offer to the person serving you a leaflet to read when things are a little quieter. With a mischievous smile, I like to add the words, 'It simply explains how Christ Jesus came into the world to save sinners . . . and I am sure you would agree that you and I qualify!' But you say something which will suit your personality.

Or, if you have had an opportunity to witness to someone about Christ, give a tract at the end of the conversation. Enclose one when writing to a friend, or paying a bill, or sending a greeting card. When salesmen come to your door be a blessing to them and give them a tract, and maybe a cup of tea.

Or, it can be a wonderful hour or two to join with some friends and go to a shopping precinct or promenade, or football ground, or wherever and give out gospel leaflets with a view to getting into conversation with those you meet. Don't stretch out your arm so that people can walk by, but go up to them, and with a friendly smile offer them the booklet. Using tracts in this way is something we all can do; it takes us onto the 'front line of battle', as we engage in seeking to point people to Christ. It could be part of the routine of the retired, the young, the lonely, or the incredibly busy. I know a pastor who goes outside his local supermarket each week to give away gospel booklets. It keeps him in regular contact with the unsaved, and releases him from the single focus of sermon preparation and delivery. For myself, I find it helpful to give away tracts like this as it serves to remind me of where people 'are at' – mostly, not interested in all things spiritual, but nevertheless, some are willing to talk and find out more.

## 2. Lose tracts

If all this seems a little too upfront for your personality, here's another idea. How many thousands of places can tracts be left? In telephone kiosks, library books, prepaid envelopes, on a bus, a train or on airplane seats, in hotel rooms, or with tips in restaurants. Then pray that the Lord would use them. You may never know the outcome, but the Lord can take hold of the scattered seed and use it for His glory.

In the context of the cancellation of debts, God gave instructions to His people, which seem interestingly applicable to the distribution of tracts.

> If there is among you a poor man of your brethren . . . you shall not harden your heart nor shut your hand from your poor brother . . . You shall surely give to him, and your heart should not be grieved when you give to him, because for this thing the LORD your God will bless you in all your works and in all to which you put your hand. For the poor will never cease from the land; therefore I command you, saying, 'You shall open your hand wide to your brother, to your poor and your needy, in your land' (Deut. 15:7,10,11).

# These boots are made for walking

So our Deputy Prime Minister, like his political prede-
cessors, wants us to leave our cars at home and walk, or
at least use public transport. There are good environ-
mental reasons for doing so. He, of course, uses transport paid for by the public and is driven by a chauffeur,
but we take the point! The Health Advisory Services tell
us that twenty minutes of brisk walking three times per
week is very good for us and, believe it or not, that is the
essence of what this article has as its aim.

Sometimes the only physical exercise I manage in the
course of a day is to walk the three or four yards to my
car. My right foot on the accelerator also gets plenty of
exercise and my jaw seems to keep quite fit. It is all too
easy to never really have contact with my neighbours. I
drive past them, there are familiar faces on the streets
nearby, but how many of their names do I actually
know, never mind their spiritual state?

## 'I'm busy: shockingly busy!'

We are aware that the most effective way of evangelism
is through 'friendship evangelism'. Sure, this is slow, and
certainly doesn't reach everyone with the gospel, but my
point is somewhat different. How many friends, neighbours and people living in the locality do we actually

know, befriend, or seek to win to Christ? Our motives, I am sure, are right. We want to win people. We pray to that end. Many of us are fully involved in evangelistic endeavours and church activities. However, as my son's answerphone jingle amusingly used to say: 'I'm busy . . . shockingly busy . . . far, far too busy for you!' We rush off to our next commitment, determined not to be late, and oblivious to the overwhelming needs of the people behind their front doors, and those we pass on the street.

We have cloistered ourselves in our cars. It is too easy, and fits perfectly into our lifestyle, to cut ourselves off from people. When I lived on a large estate on the outskirts of Leeds, the local Anglican clergyman, who was by no means an evangelical, taught me a lesson. He used to cycle everywhere on an old sit-up-and-beg bicycle. Going up the main street he would see people, brake, stop and chat for a few minutes. I think his pastoral visitation was done that way. Through these means he met and was involved with people. Then I heard of a group of people who had started a church by walking and getting to know people. Following the same route, at the same time each day, they got to know shoppers, gardeners, postmen, maintenance workers and the like. Slowly they got to know them, talk and befriend them, getting to know about their family, occupation, religion, before sharing Christ with them.

We need to remind ourselves of our Lord and Saviour. What was Jesus doing when He saw the widow of Nain whose son had just died? Jesus was in the thick of things when blind Bartimaeus called out, and when the ten lepers came to Him, and when He spotted Zacchaeus. Would Cleopas and his friend (wife?) ever forget their momentous walk from Jerusalem to Emmaus? Jesus was out and about with people where He could be involved in people-orientated ministry.

**First steps**

Naturally, there are physical benefits to walking. It is good to just amble and take in the surroundings, enjoying conversation and the fresh air. My pleading though is that by walking we can take a first step towards evangelising people around about us. It may be that you walk with tracts to give to open up conversations, or that you will prayerfully seek to build up lasting contacts and friendships. There may be a neighbour or friend with whom you could regularly go walking. But walk prayerfully, and ask the Lord to lead you to the right people. If you are so English that you find it hard to speak without an introduction, ask the Lord to be the invisible but very present Friend, whose desire is that you should meet someone He is concerned for. Purposeful walking can in itself be a ministry. Many have found that seeking to speak to at least one soul each day about Christ has been a great blessing to them, as well as to those they meet.

Mrs Sienko was my father's secretary for twenty-five years. When I was newly converted, I tried to witness to her, but remembering her reaction, I think my manner was not very endearing! It was Boxing Day, years later, and I had walked down to the newsagent to buy the paper. Walking back, Mrs Sienko and I saw each other across the road. We were going in the same direction so began walking together. As I was trying to nudge the subject of the conversation onto spiritual things, she told me that her son had 'become a born-again Christian'. When I found that she was delighted about this, I asked if she had ever trusted Christ in the same way. She replied, 'No, but I would love to.' Within days, she had been converted and now faithfully attends our church. We saw each other . . . walking. If I'd been secluded in my car, I would have probably driven by without even noticing her.

Life is too short to rush through without the eternal work of being involved in meeting and reaching people. Therefore, as well as helping the environment (God's world) and keeping fit, leave the car in the drive, go for a walk and meet people who need to meet the Lord.

# 20/20 vision[20]

Life itself is a great teacher. For twenty years I was involved in evangelism while a student and then a teacher. Now, for the last twenty years I have worked full-time as an itinerant evangelist. I have had many teachers, and many lessons. They are too numerous to completely list, but here are a number of themes condensed to give an idea of some of the things the Lord, and others, have been teaching me.

1. *I have learned my own unworthiness to do anything that will count for eternity.* C.S. Lewis, who once said that one out of every three of his thoughts was sinful, expressed exactly how I feel – he had found out ludicrous and terrible things about his own character. I genuinely believe that anything accomplished for the glory of God has been of His doing and of His grace, and nothing to do with anything good in me.

2. *I have learned that ministry cannot be done alone.* I could not have done even a tiny proportion of the work without a devoted wife, understanding children, wise parents, and a host of others who have been great friends and helpers. People have supported me, prayed for me, given to the work, shown hospitality, and sacrificially helped in numerous

ways. We all need each other, and I have been at the receiving end of the kindnesses and generosity of so many people. Service for the Lord is teamwork of His people using their varied talents and gifts for His glory. The church is a body with many members.

3. *I have learned that though I imagined I would stay with certain activities permanently, God alters our agenda.* Although I greatly value the opportunities they provided, and pray for their continuing usefulness, the Lord trimmed and focused my work and areas of involvement. Those ministries have gone on without me, proving that I am dispensable! For me, the Lord has used health issues to capture my attention and redirect me. I trust that in all my work, the emphasis continues to be 'this one thing I do . . .'

4. *I have learned that God uses people who disagree with me.* There are basic beliefs and doctrines which I believe to be absolute essentials for salvation and Christian fellowship. As well, there are places I will not go, and things I cannot do if I am to maintain a clear conscience and close walk with the Lord. However, I am aware that not all my brothers and sisters in Christ see eye-to-eye on these and on some of the periphery issues of Christian beliefs. God blesses and uses them, and who am I to write them off, or to distance them from my heart? I may not choose to work closely with them, but I love them as brothers and sisters in the Lord.

5. *I have learned that the Lord has His people.* Repeatedly I have been struck by meeting saintly people, whether in the UK, Europe, USA, India or

Nicaragua. They may never have their names in lights or headlines, and in one hundred years from now will be forgotten on earth. Yet they are godly, loving, eternally minded people of integrity. They are the salt of the earth. They are scattered in different countries and settings, are of varying ages and backgrounds, but they are impressive. They are found at their church prayer meetings, and in the place of devotion each day. There are deeply spiritual pastors, leaders and everyday believers who labour in the Word and prayer, who 'know their stuff' and want to be a blessing to others. They are a blessing to me.

I deeply appreciate the vision, selflessness and kindness of each person who has worked to open a door of opportunity for me, by creating evangelistic events, or recommending my name. These people have enabled me to share the gospel in many more places than would otherwise have been possible. I am hugely indebted to these partners in the work.

6. *I have learned that there is in our land a famine for the Word of God*. The great need is to get the Bible message out, whether on church notice boards, through literature, public ministry and personal conversations. As a nation, we seem to have turned from the true and living God to idols, whether they are the soaps, the stars, soccer or sex. The media is about life without God, and this has been imbibed by the nation whose greatest need is to hear the Word of God.

7. *I have learned that virtually everyone I meet is hurting in one way or another*. They may be busy, affluent and apparently happy, but underneath there are issues

which gnaw away at them. Both Christians and the unconverted usually need to be treated with gentleness and meekness. The Scottish theologian, John Watson, said, 'Be kind; you do not know what battles people are fighting.' He was right. I heard the Ulster preacher, Willie Mullen say that each Saturday, when preparing his sermon for the next day, he prayed 'For a word of encouragement for the saints.' I present the Christ who loves, as well as the God who judges, the Jesus who lovingly appealed to all who are weary and heavy laden saying, 'Come unto me.'

8. *I have seen a diminishing of confidence in evangelistic preaching*. I fear that because we have not seen great reaping in our land for some decades, we have lowered our expectation and have become non-evangelistic evangelicals. We have evangelical churches that don't effectively evangelise; 'evangelistic' activities where the gospel is not proclaimed, and Bible teaching which is never gospel preaching. Sadly, few churches are organising missions, and yet they can be so fruitful and such a blessing. We have a responsibility to those 'across the street and around the world', as Steve Green sings.

9. *I have learned that as Christians we are only touching the surface of the need*. We are aware that church membership in the UK is haemorrhaging. People in their twenties and thirties are not filling pews, and hundreds of thousands of teenagers are not hearing the most relevant, urgent message they could ever hear. So much of our evangelism focuses on our friends, but who reaches those who do not know a Christian? There are people who go to bed when I

get up, and get up when I go to bed. Who reaches them? Who reaches the thousands of people who cram the nightclubs every weekend, or who live on council estates where many Christians choose not to live, or who never go to university, or who never leave their Muslim, Hindu or Buddhist communities?

10. *I have seen that evangelistic events that focus on a particular type of person*, e.g. men, women, young people, lawyers, diabetics, international students, etc., are often best at getting in a larger proportion of unconverted people.

11. *I have learned that although we are not living in times of revival or even great reaping, nevertheless, people are being converted.* I find that day after day I meet with people with whom I get into conversation about the things of God, and they want to know more. Time and again, I move away from what started as an inconsequential conversation thinking, 'Amazing! How did that start? What a wonderful opportunity I have just had!' Through church work and personal work, through courses such as *Christianity Explored*, literature, schools work and summer teams, people are being saved. It might be that in time there will be a greater harvest; but until then I want to dedicate myself afresh to the task of proclaiming Christ and Him crucified, to every creature I possibly can.

I thank God for the last twenty years. He has opened doors of opportunity and has answered so many prayers. I praise Him for all that has been accomplished through literature, tape – and now digital – recordings, and the spoken word. I am aware that anything accomplished has been but a drop in the ocean, and much of my work is very small. If God continues to allow me to minister, with His grace and for His glory, I want to preach Christ crucified, to those who feel the message is foolishness or a stumbling-block. It may be that they too may discover that Christ is the power of God and the wisdom of God.

Meanwhile, I trust I will always have an attitude that accepts when I have made mistakes, and is teachable. Only then will I continue to learn. Only then will God continue to work within me, but that is another subject.

# ENDNOTES

1 Biography of Rev. Sisag Manoogian, *Out of the Ark*, Rhoda G. Carswell, is available from me.
2 I have put the Litany on the www.theeangelist.org.uk website if you want to download it.
3 A. Carmichael, *Mountain Breezes: the collected poems of Amy Carmichael* (Christian Literature Crusade, 1999), 119.
4 P. St. John, *Biography of R. Hudson Pope* (Milton Keynes: Scripture Union), 106.
5 D. Smart, *Kingdom Builders* (Milton Keynes: Authentic Media, 2005).
6 E. Wiesel, *Night* (London: Penguin, 1981), 9.
7 D. Greenwell, 'I am not skilled to understand' in *Songs of Salvation* (1873).
8 H. Roseveare, *Digging Ditches* (Tain: Christian Focus, 2005), 77.
9 John Bunyan, *Pilgrim's Progress* (London: Penguin – reprinted in Penguin Classics 1986. Reprinted with revisions 1987).
10 'Ebenezer' means 'hitherto, the Lord has led me' – see 1 Samuel 4:1.
11 A. Carmichael, *Mountain Breezes: the collected poems of Amy Carmichael* (Christian Literature Crusade, 1999), 260.
12 J.C. Ryle, *Christ Crucified*.
13 C.H. Spurgeon, *The Tender Mercy of Our God* (1886).
14 Portia Nelson, from *There's a Hole in my Sidewalk* (Hillsboro, Oregon: Beyond Words Publishing Inc., 1993).
15 W. Wordsworth, *The Excursion* (1814).

16 J. Edwards, *Sinners in the Hands of an Angry God* (Wheaton, Illinois: Whitaker House, 1997).

17 B. Lloyd-Jones, *Memories of Sandfields* (Edinburgh: Banner of Truth, 1983), 85.

18 D. Larsen, *The Evangelism Mandate* (Leicester: Crossway Books, 1992), 85.

19 If you would like a sample pack of tracts written by Roger Carswell, please contact Print by Design.
e-mail:chris@printbydesign.co.uk.

20 Written in June 2003.